Student's Companion to the World Wide Web

Social Sciences and Humanities Resources

Jim Millhorn

The Scarecrow Press, Inc.
Lanham, Maryland, and London
1999

SCARECROW PRESS, INC.

Published in the United States of America
by Scarecrow Press, Inc.
4720 Boston Way, Lanham, Maryland 20706
http://www.scarecrowpress.com

4 Pleydell Gardens, Folkestone
Kent CT20 2DN, England

British Library Cataloguing in Publication Information Available

Library of Congress Cataloging-in-Publication Data

Millhorn, Jim, 1953–
    Student's companion to the World Wide Web : social sciences and
humanities resources / Jim Millhorn.
        p.   cm.
    ISBN 0-8108-3680-7 (pbk.)
    1. Social sciences—Computer network resources Directories. 2.
Humanities—Computer network resources Directories. 3. World Wide
Web (Information retrieval system) I. Title.
H61.95.M55   1999
025.06′3—dc21   99-41057
                                                        CIP

⊖™ The paper used in this publication meets the minimum requirements of
American National Standard for Information Sciences—Permanence of
Paper for Printed Library Materials, ANSI/NISO Z39.48–1992.
Manufactured in the United States of America.

Contents

English Literature 77

Foreign Languages 83

Music and Dance 88

Philosophy and Religion 94

About the Author 101

Introduction

There is an ever growing proliferation of sites and information sources posted on the world wide web. The fact is that this dense mass of data is crowding out quality sites, and hence making them difficult to locate. This book proposes to examine only a small corner of this vast undergrowth. The focus here is on outstanding academic and scholarly sites for students in the social sciences and humanities.

As a librarian, I have noticed students time and again struggle to extract useful information from the web. The students clearly sense the potential import of the web, yet are not at all clear about the best means or methods for exploiting this potential. Their searches are most often very broad and what valuable information they elicit is located more through happenstance rather than systematic inquiry. Indeed, there are definite limits to how systematically the web can be explored, in that by its very nature it is unregulated and amorphous. On the other hand, some sites are clearly better than others and some others are manifestly superior, especially in the academic realm. By concentrating on choice academic sites students will learn to better tap in to the web as an instrument of knowledge and instruction.

There is a plethora of Internet guides on the market that tout the virtues of cyberspace and offer instructions for the mechanics of navigating the net, sending E-mail and the like. This is not such a book. It is accepted from the outset that the web is not only a legitimate medium of scholarly discourse, but that it will occupy an increasingly prominent position in academia. The proof of this proposition is not argued theoretically but offered concretely as evidenced by the many sites described below. Moreover, it is assumed that the student already has a passing knowledge of how to operate a web browser such as Netscape or Microsoft Explorer and some experience navigating the web via a search engine. In other words, space will not be devoted to explaining the functions of a browser toolbar, or how to place bookmarks, or other purely mechanical features of employing a browser. Rather emphasis is placed on in-depth exploration of individual academic disciplines.

The outline of the book is simple. The first three chapters focus on common reference sources, search engines, and what I have termed meta-subject guides. The remainder of the book is roughly divided in-two with the first half dedicated to social science disciplines and the second to humanities. Each half opens with a chapter on broad, general sites aimed at the whole of the social sciences and humanities, respectively. These initial chapters are followed by an alphabetized sequence of chapters featuring individual disciplines, such that the humanities division begins with art and concludes with philosophy and religion. The first site at the head of each chapter was selected according to its comprehensiveness in canvassing the entire disciplinary field. Often this was a tough choice, and alternative or competing sites are frequently noted. Following the comprehensive site there are number of sites that focus on and delineate the subdisciplines which comprise the field. The effect is much the same as if browsing a college catalog. First there are the broad introductory courses, which are then succeeded by more specialized subdisciplines. For instance, the chapter on psychology opens with a comprehensive site and then advances to the subdisciplines, such as neuropsychology, cognitive psychology, experimental psychology, clinical psychology, social psychology, psychoanalysis, and so forth. The overall aim of this organizational structure is to open the broadest possible purview the web offers on a specific discipline, while at the same time rigorously limiting the number of featured sites. The one thing students do not need is to be overwhelmed by an endless sea of links and addresses.

The selection criteria for the inclusion of sites are also quite simple. First and foremost, sites were chosen on the basis of their information content and the quality of their scholarship. This involves not only the quantity and value of the information posted, but also how effectively it is packaged and organized.

Obviously, if the information is ill organized and difficult to locate it detracts from the value of the site. Moreover, all noteworthy sites contain a fair amount of original information and commentary, and a few are wholly original in content. Second, it is equally important for a site to have intelligently selected linkages to other sites of note. In this way the creator of a site helps illustrate what worthwhile projects other colleagues are pursuing on the web. Experienced web searchers in the academic realm find a very high degree of self-referentiality in that colleagues are uniformly generous in acknowledging one another's work. It is also owing to this generosity in citing and referring to one another that even a limited number of sites can open a broad window to the web. Third, it is absolutely critical that posted information is current and frequently updated. It is easy to recognize a web site that is not continually refreshed in that there will be an annoying number of dead links that lead to nowhere. Dead links will always be a problem to a certain degree but vigilant maintenance can keep them to a minimum.

The web is notoriously volatile and un-stable. Web sites appear and disappear on a daily basis. Equally disconcerting are constant changes in servers, domains and addresses. The best sites leave a forwarding link to the new address but this is not universal. There is a preference throughout the book for estab-lished academic figures not only because of their mastery of their particular field, but also for the reason they tend to be more stable. Graduate students have posted some fine web sites, and a number of them are included, but they tend to move on and get involved in other projects. Consequently, I have been somewhat shy of featuring graduate student's work unless I felt confident of their continued maintenance. Whatever the domain, good web sites indicate the last time they were updated. A number of the best web sites I have visited are updated on virtually a weekly basis. One of the most exciting aspects of the web is its dynamism wherein one must remain ever vigilant to the emergence of new sites and information. The web is anything but static.

It is important not to overstate the virtues of the web. In my mind it is no substitute for print resources and other customary media. In certain areas it excels, such as in furnishing reference information, and statistical, and quan-titative data. It is equally indisputable that like all things new and experimental it is prone to faddishness and ephemera parading as learning. Despite the problems and posturing it is com-mendable how a number of dedicated aca-demics have grasped the power of the web and incorporated it in their teaching. The bene-ficiaries are not only their direct students but also that growing community of web users sifting the net for knowledge and instruction.

Reference

Reference works, or more precisely ready reference works, are those tools that either furnish quick access to information, or direct one to resources that can provide the information in question. Examples of the most heavily employed ready reference resources are dictionaries, encyclopedias, almanacs and the like. The web is an ideal means of efficiently furnishing such information, and at present there are hundreds of different types of reference works available online. This chapter will focus on the main categories of ready reference, and also highlight a few outstanding examples.

Virtual Ready Reference Collection

http://web.lwc.edu/administrative/library/refu.htm

This handy site is maintained by Calvin Boyer, a librarian at Longwood College, Farmville, Virginia. The site furnishes a good one-stop source for reference. It features thirty-five separate information categories listed alphabetically. The categories range from *Acronyms and Abbreviations* to *Zip Codes*. Each of the categories highlights a select group of resources, such as *Consumer Information* links to the *Consumer Information Center, Consumer World, Edmund's Automobile Buyer's Guide, Internet Mall, Kelly's Blue Book, Product Review Net* and *U.S. Consumer Gateway*. What I particularly like about this site is its selectivity and ease of navigation. On the other hand, there are several instances of huge reference collections posted on the web, and if that is more to your liking, try the **Internet Public Reference Desk** at **http:// www.ipl.org/ref/**, or the very crowded **My Virtual Reference Desk** at **http://www.refdesk.com**.

WWWebster Dictionary

http://www.m-w.com/dictionary.htm

The most essential reference work that comes to mind is an English dictionary. Merriam-Webster generously placed the tenth edition of the hallowed Webster's dictionary on the web. It is very simple and efficient, and it operates through a search form positioned on the main page. The dictionary furnishes not only the varying definitions of a word but also offers a brief etymology and a pronunciation key. Terms that are boldface within the text indicate extra entries that can be searched. In addition, a thesaurus is packaged with the dictionary so there is an automatic means of extending a search. There is, of course, a scad of online dictionaries available over the web, an impressive selection of which are posted at Professor Robert Beard's **A Web of On-Line Dictionaries** at **http://www.facstaff.bucknell.edu/~rbeard/diction.html**. The Internet is an area of the language witnessing constant change. A good site for keeping tabs on the new argot is **http:// www.netlingo.com**.

http://www.encyclopedia.com

Next to a dictionary, the most basic type of reference work is an encyclopedia. This site features a complete online version of the third edition of *The Concise Columbia Electronic Encyclopedia* and is maintained by the Infonautics Corporation of Boston. The entries are not as long, nor as comprehensive, as commercial or fee based encyclopedias such as the *Britannica*, but nonetheless there are more than 17,000 entries. Although the entries are brief, they are well informed and thoughtfully cross referenced. A search form is placed at the head of the main page, and there is also an alphabetic browse feature. Two other encyclopedias worth investigating are Microsoft's **Encarta Concise Encyclopedia** at **http:// encarta.msn.com/EncartaHome.asp** and the

Free Internet Encyclopedia, drawn exclusively from Internet resources, at **http://clever.net/cam/encyclopedia.html**.

http://www.biography.com

Closely related to encyclopedias are biographical dictionaries. This site maintained by A&E features over 20,000 biographies largely drawn from the *Cambridge Encyclopedia Database* and *The Cambridge Dictionary of American Biography*. Each entry offers a brief summary of the figure's accomplishments, and there are solid cross references. An interesting and also remarkably informative biographical resource is **The Nobel Prize Internet Archive** at **http://nobelprizes.com/nobel/nobel.html**.

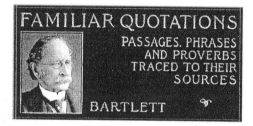

Bartlett's Familiar Quotations
http://www.cc.columbia.edu/acis/bartleby/bartlett

This site, hosted by Columbia University, offers an ingenious online version of this classic reference work. Alas, this is not the latest version, but rather the ninth edition of 1901. Even then, however, the work weighs in at 1,158 pages. There is a keyword search engine at the top of the page, and a chronological list of all the authors. For instance, clicking on Chaucer retrieves fifty-eight items with accompanying notes. Shakespeare is meted out with special distinction, in that each of the plays is allocated a separate slot. Although the ancients and continental Europe are represented, the lion's share of the database is absorbed by British authors.

There is also a good collection of passages culled from the Bible. Another good site for quotations that links to a number of different sources is **The Quotations Page** at http://www.starlingtech.com/quotes.

Information Please: Your Ultimate Fact Finder
http://www.infoplease.com

"Information Please" started as a radio quiz show back in the late 1930s and has evolved into a dynamic publishing firm best known for it justly renowned *Information Please Almanac*. In any case, "Information Please" on the web represents a mammoth compilation of several annual almanacs and dictionaries under a single roof. There are literally thousands of useful nuggets of information posted here. The site is divided into a number of topical categories including *World*, *United States*, *Living*, *Sports*, *People*, *Society*, *Entertainment*, *Business & Economy*, and *Science and Technology*. Each of these categories is divided and subdivided into a number of other topical areas. Hence, despite the mass of available information, the site is relatively easy to navigate. A great deal of the material is statistical in nature, but there is also a good deal of narrative. The site performs as an excellent fact checker. Another basic reference work that focuses just on the US is the Census Bureau's abridged version of the **Statistical Abstract of the United States** at **http://www.census.gov/statab/www**. For foreign nationalities, use the CIA's excellent **World Factbook http:// www.odci. gov/cia/publications/factbook**.

Hotlinks to Newspapers Online
http://www.naa.org/hotlinks/index.asp

There is always a ready demand for current news. This particular site, hosted by the Newspaper Association of America, features online access to 785 dailies. There is a map of the nation at the center of the main page on which one can click and select a specific state. For instance, clicking on Illinois retrieves 27 newspapers representing the major metropolitan areas. There are additional categories for *Canadian Newspapers*, *Collectives* (Gannet, Hearst, etc.), *Weeklies*, *Business Papers*, *Alternative Press*, *Internationals*, *Press Associations*, etc. All of the major television and radio networks also have a strong web presence. Of particular note, for news at least, is **CNN Interactive** at **http://www.cnn.com**.

http://www.anywho.com

The flexible search capabilities and massive blocks of information that the web manipulates have made it an ideal place for posting directories. There is a lot of competition in the field, and certainly no one directory can claim to be comprehensive. However, among the very best is the "Any Who Directory Service," underwritten by AT&T. One can search for telephone numbers for either people or businesses from over 90 million listings. The search form includes name of the individual or firm, street address, city, zipcode and state. Items retrieved from the search include not only phone numbers, but also detailed maps of how to locate the persons or places in question. This is a neat service.

If one wants to sample a number of different directories, try **Telephone Directories on the Web** at **http://www.Contractjobs.com/tel**. In my experience locating Internet addresses via a web search is a much more iffy proposition. If the address is a university student or faculty member, or tied to a business, the best route is to search the internal directories of that given institution or enterprise. On

the other hand, if all the information you have is a name, organization, or domain, try the **Internet Address Finder** at **http://www.iaf.net/**.

http://www.mapsonus.com

As the chapter on Geography will bear out, maps and geographic information have made wondrous strides under the aegis of the web. This marvelous site comes courtesy of Switchboard and lives up to its promise that it makes "navigation simple all across the United States." From the main page, select either the *Maps* or *Routes* button. The former requires a street address, city and state, and a zip code, if handy. The search retrieves a remarkably detailed map with the capability to zoom in and out. The latter offers separate forms for the start and end of the route and furnishes not only a precise map of the route, but also provides accurate turn-by-turn directions from point A to point B. If you have not tried a web mapping service previously you are sure to be impressed. Another quality mapping site that is **Mapquest** at **http:// www.mapquest.com**. One additional type of directory or directional aid is the zip code. The Postal Service has an easy and convenient **Zip +4 Code Lookup** at **http://www.usps.gov/ncsc/**

American Universities

http://www.clas.ufl.edu/CLAS/american-universities.html

Students always have questions about the programs and course selections at other universities, and with the advent of the web, it is much easier to provide that information. Virtually all colleges and universities now have a web presence and, indeed, most institutions put a good deal of care and thought into the layout and organization of their site. After all, an increasing number of prospective students first contact with an institution is via the web.

This site maintained by Professor Mike Conlon, Department of Statistics, University of Florida, offers a highly comprehensive directory to colleges, universities, and graduate programs in the United States. The schools are displayed in simple alphabetic order. Conlon also provides a separate set of indexes to community colleges, and Canadian and international universities. Another site that offers links to a vast array of academic, public and national libraries is **Libweb** at **http://sunsite. berkeley.edu/Libweb**.

1998-99 Occupational Outlook Handbook ⓑⓢ

http://stats.bls.gov/ocohome.htm

Students have an obvious interest in the job prospects of any major they choose. One of the most reliable and established sources is the above handbook, published under the auspices of the Bureau of Labor Statistics.The online version of the handbook is an exact reproduction of the print publication. It can be searched by keyword and also possesses a detailed index including broad occupational clusters. Each profession is furnished with a substantial narrative, the outline of which consists of sections devoted to *Nature of the Work*; *Working Conditions*; *Employment*; *Training, Other Qualifications, and Advancement*; *Job Outlook*; *Earnings*; *Related Occupations*; and *Sources of Additional Information*. All in all, the handbook ranks job prospects for individual fields and is good to consult before selecting a major.

There are also a growing number of web sites aimed at recruitment and hiring and advance general advice on landing a job. Some of the sites list thousands of positions and offer interesting comparisons of salaries, benefits, and the like. One of the best employment related sites is the National Association of Colleges and Employers, **The Catapult on JOB WEB** at **http://www.jobweb.org/catapult/**. Another site worth exploring is **Quintissential Careers** at **http://www.quintcareers.com/**.

The Universal Currency Converter™

http://www.xe.net/currency

megaConverter

http://www.megaconverter.com

A frequent inquiry which the web does an outstanding job of answering are questions dealing with measurements and conversion from one standard to another. For instance, "The Universal Currency Converter" gives up to the minute exchange rates on every currency one could imagine. The main page features two forms from which to select currencies, say American dollars for Polish zlotys, and then with a click an exchange rate is posted.

Another type of conversion deals with weights and other units of measure. The "mega Converter" boasts an astonishing thirty-six separate measurement categories including area, density, energy, length, mass and weight, speed, temperature, time, volume, etc. Most conversion questions can be answered at this single stop. On the other hand, if the question is a bit more exotic and specifically deals with foreign measures say, converting ängstroms to inches, then try the Berlin based **Conversion of Units** page at **http://www.chemie.fu-berlin. de/chemistry/general/units_en.html**. If one prefers a printed list of unit relationships see, Stephen Phillips **Unit Conversion** page at **http://www.soton.ac.uk/~scp93ch/refer/con vfact.html**.

Karla's Guide to Citation Style Guides

http://bailiwick.lib.uiowa.edu/ journalism/cite.html

One problem arising from the mass of information available over the Internet is how to properly cite this material in papers and publications. Karla Tonella, affiliated with the University of Iowa Libraries, has assembled a useful list of diverse citation guidelines, including the American Psychological Association, Chicago Manual of Style, Council of Biology Editors, Modern Language Associa-tion and Turabian. In addition to citation pro-tocols there are references to copyright issues and more general questions of writing style. For a succinct summary of divergent citation forms, see also **Style Manuals** at **http://www.lib. muohio.edu/~shocker/man/style.html**.

http://cirrus.sprl.umich.edu/wxnet

One question that invariably crops up concerns the weather. Because of the broad interest in the weather there is tremendous competition for bragging rights, and as a consequence there are a number of excellent sites featuring current weather information. "WeatherNet" is hosted by the University of Michigan, and furnishes meteorological data on a global basis. One can hone in not only on local weather, but also tap into regional and continental trends and projections.

On the main page, under the heading *FastForecast*, there is a search form that searches either by city, state, country, or zip code. Moreover, there are separate categories for radar and satellite images, maps, software, storm warnings, ski reports, and a huge index of over 300 related weather sites. Other web sites worth checking out are the **Weather Channel** at **http://www.weather.com** and **AC-CUWEATHER** at **http://www.accuweather. com**.

Search Engines

Search engines attempt to organize the mass of disparate data posted on the Internet into some coherent fashion and as such form a fundamental aspect of the architecture of the web. Indeed, it would hardly be possible to navigate the web without search engines. Anyone with even a passing familiarity with the web is aware of major players in the field, such as Yahoo and AltaVista. This chapter proposes a brief overview of some of the more popular and powerful search engines. It should be noted, however, that what is offered here does not constitute an endorsement of any particular search engine, or search engines in general.

Despite the indispensability of search engines they have inherent limitations. First, no search engine is capable of encompassing all the material posted on the Internet, or the web for that matter. There is simply too much stuff for any machine to track down. Second, the ability of search engines to discriminate in terms of quality is very limited, and this is particularly crucial when applied to academic sites. After all, if search engines could perform at high levels of precision and could distinguish choice sites from also-rans then there would be no purpose for this book. Instead of focusing on quality, search engines rely on evaluations (largely statistical) of relevancy. In the broadest terms the difference between search engines is determined by the way they compute or assess relevancy. It is owing to these divergent standards that an identical search conducted on two separate search engines can yield wildly different results. In any case, the aim here is not to belittle search engines but to make a realistic assessment of what they can and cannot accomplish.

There are many sites that test and evaluate search engines, but this one stands clearly above the fray. This site maintained by Danny Sullivan, an Internet consultant and journalist for Mecklermedia, offers a multitude of ways of looking at search engines. The search engine arena changes almost daily, and unlike a number of one-shot search engine evaluations this one is updated regularly. The site is divided into five sections: *Webmaster's Guide to Search Engines*; *Search Engine Facts and Fun*; *Search Engine Status Reports*; *Search Engine Resources*; and *Search Engine Report Newsletter*.

The first section is oriented more toward the specialist and web sophisticate, but the remainder offer a host of useful information. For instance, under the "facts and fun" section, there are numerous categories that outline the major search engines and offer reviews, recommendations, and detailed tutorials so as to maximize the search potential of each of the engines. On the other hand, the section denoted as "status reports" offers in depth comparative analyses of the performance of each of the search engines, and specifies how the individual engines search and examine the web. Finally, the last section, devoted to the "newsletter," offers free monthly updates of search engine news. A good article by David Brake, published in the *New Scientist* of June 1997, points out a few of the search engine hazards. **Lost in Cyberspace** is at **http://www. newscientist.com/keysites/networld/lost. html**. For those who want to sample a massive array of search engines try the remarkable **Internet Sleuth** at **http://www.isleuth.com**. This site encompasses more than 3,000 searchable databases and breaks them down into relevant subject areas such as economics, literature, and so forth.

http://searchenginewatch.com

http://www.yahoo.com

This is one of the oldest, most popular, and most heavily used of all the search engines. It was initially developed by a couple of Stanford graduate students in electrical engineering, David Filo and Jerry Yang, and once its name started circulating on the web its growth accelerated in exponential terms. In the strict sense of the term Yahoo is not a search engine, but more like a directory. There is a form at the top of the main page that searches the entire database, yet just below are listed a number of broad subject categories in which major sites or sites with a lot of hits are classified. In the majority of cases, it is recommended to search or browse under the subject categories. Retrieval of items tends to be more precise that way.

There are fourteen subject divisions in all, ranging alphabetically from *Arts & Humanities* to *Society & Culture*. Each of the categories in turn is divvied up into a number of subcategories. For instance, clicking on *Social Sciences* retrieves a directory of subject headings ranging from *Anthropology and Archaeology* to *Women's Studies*. The *Sociology* category indicates that there are 360 links listed, and clicking on it opens a number of options. First, there is a form under *Sociology* that allows searching within that category. Second, just below the form, there are a number of subdivisions listed such as *Criminology, Demography, Social Psychology, Urban Studies*, etc. Third, following on the heels of the subdivisions is a highly select list of preferred sites. Each link has a brief annotation. It is not clear how sites are selected, but most of the links are interesting, if not necessarily the best available.

In any case, it is clear that Yahoo fruitfully combines the elements of a full-blown search engine and a more discriminating directory. An important feature that Yahoo shares with most of the search engines is a set of tools and techniques that allow for refined and sophisticated searching. Unfortunately, most users fail to take adequate account of these tools, and Yahoo does not make it all that obvious how to unearth instructions for more precise searching. However, there is a wealth of information at **http://search.yahoo.com/search/help**. A brief perusal of these pages makes it clear that there are many options aside from simply typing an unadorned word or phrase into a form and

hoping the yield more or less faithfully matches the intent of the search. Much of Yahoo's populairty stems from its outward simplicity, but do not sell the search engine short, because it is also capable of a high degree of sophistication.

http://www.altavista.com

AltaVista is among the fastest of the search engines, yet at the same time indexes more pages, or simply comprehends more data, than virtually any other search engine. One recent innovation is that AltaVista has adopted a semi-directory structure in that under the category of *Zones* they have established broad divisions for *Careers, Entertainment, Finance, Health, News by ABC*, and *Travel*. However, the strength of AltaVista consists in its ability to scan an immense amount of information in a short time.

AltaVista is not the place to conduct a broad general search. Most often general searches will result in a massive overload to the tune of thousands of hits. Fortunately, clicking on *Help* from the main page offers a number of different strategies and tips on how to refine and sharpen searches. It is highly recommended to review the help screens before initiating a search. AltaVista is a powerful search tool, yet to take full advantage of it requires a very sharp and precise search strategy.

http://www.hotbot.com

HotBot is sponsored by the Internet journal *Wired*, and in terms of size and scope rivals AltaVista. Although it does not share the exposure or popular appeal of AltaVista, on a number of tests it has consistently received high ratings. These favorable ratings are attributable to the main page's highly articulated graphical interface.

Unlike most search engines, there is not a single search form, but rather a series of forms that allow one to progressively refine a search. For instance, a search can be limited to those just recently posted, or qualified by domain such as educational, commercial, governmental or foreign. Moreover, searches can be restriced to pages that include video, audio, and images, and there is also an advanced search form under the heading *More Search Options*. The search forms are supplemented by a command driven search syntax allowing for a variety of complex searches. In order to locate this search syntax click, on *Help* and then *Advanced Search Features*. In addition, there is a browsable directory structure, but it is really secondary to the strengths of the search engine. HotBot is the engine of choice for those seeking to test and extend searching skills.

http://infoseek.com

Infoseek was founded by Steven Kirsch in 1994 and has established an admirable record for innovation. On the surface, Infoseek looks very similar to Yahoo. It has a directory structure divied into seventeen separate categories, dubbed channels, ranging from *Automotive* to *Women's*. On the other hand, Infoseek is a true search engine with vast resources, and one is certainly not bound to the directory structure. Just above the search form is a bar denoted *Tips*. Clicking on the bar retrieves a search menu of search instructions which is easy to follow, and also highlights the versatility of the search engine. There is also a bar for a highly articulated *Advanced Search*.

However, in my view, the strongest feature of Infoseek compared to other search engines is its treatment of academia. For instance, click on the *Education* channel. This retrieves a page with a number of headings. Of particular note is the heading *Education sites*, and the subcategory *Fields of study*. Clicking on the latter

retrieves a directory of eleven topical areas ranging from, *Environment* to *Social Sciences*. Each of the areas lists relevant disciplines so that for example under *Social Sciences* are located sections devoted to *Anthropology, Cognitive Science, Geography, Linguistics, Political Science, Psychology, Sociology, Speech & Communications, UrbanStudies,* and *Women's studies*. Each of these fields, in turn, is divided into subfields with an attached set of well chosen links. For those just venturing out, Infoseek is a good vehicle to tap in to the academic potential of the web.

http://www.excite.com

Excite is a massive search engine/directory in the same vein as Infoseek. It was founded by six Stanford graduates in 1995 and has consistently ranked as one of the best all purpose search engines. It has so many features, including news, stocks, sports scores, chat, horoscopes, etc. that the main page looks a little too busy and crowded. However, the mainstays of the site are the search form at the top of the page and the directory structure just below.

The form includes a good help screen, dubbed *Search Tips*, and an advanced *Power Search* feature. The directory boasts seventeen categories ranging from *Autos* to *Travel*. The category reserved for *Education* does include a bar for *Fields of Study*, which covers the major academic disciplines. Although there are many interesting and useful items located here, the academic fields are not as clearly and thoughtfully represented as in Infoseek. In general, Excite has a more commercial and popular culture feel to it. Another major search engine that also warrants mention is **Lycos** at **http://www. lycos.com**. A relative newcomer to the search engine field that looks promising is **Northern Light** at **http://www.northernlight.com**.

http://www.dogpile.com

Dogpile is a creature of another stripe in that it is a compendium of search engines or rather searches multiple search engines simultaneously. Dogpile clearly reveals how different search engines scan the web in very different ways. No two search engines retrieve the same results, and more often than not they are not even close. All in all, Dogpile is comprised of twenty-five search engines and databases, including major figures in the field such as Yahoo, Excite, Lycos, AltaVista and Infoseek. A sample search on the phrase "psychological tests" was conducted, and the results amply confirmed the lack of consistency between the databases. Although all the search engines were able to locate numerous sites, I found Infoseek did the best job in honing in on relevant sites. Dogpile does allow for some advanced syntax search features and can also be customized to where the user sets the order in which each particular search engine is activated. However,better results generally will be achieved by tapping into each search engine individually, especially in terms of taking full advantage of search options. Not all of the options of Excite, Yahoo etc. are available on Dogpile. Dogpile can achieve a number of interesting effects, but it should not be the search engine of choice for everyday purposes. For links and a solid review of search engines comparable to Dogpile see **Multiple Search Engines** at **http://www. notess.com**.

Meta-Subject Guides

Meta-subject guides are searchable databases that share a close affinity with search engines. Yahoo, Excite, Infoseek, etc. are, after all, organized around subject directories, yet what we are dubbing meta-subject guides offer both something more and less than search engines proper. The outstanding trait of meta-subject guides is that they are evaluative and critical. In other words, meta-subject guides are highly selective and attempt to rank various sites according to topic. The criteria by which sites are evaluated and included vary from one meta-subject guide to another. Some meta-subject guides are more academic in orientation than others, and some are more purely popular. Although meta-subject guides furnish links to individual sites, their primary focus is on providing coverage of specific disciplines or subdisciplines. The meta-subject guides offer less than the major search engines in that they are not nearly as comprehensive, and do not include near the number of linkages. In sum, the meta-subject guides offer a more focused and concentrated vision of the web, especially in the way they attempt to highlight the crown jewels of the web. In this regard, the meta-subject guides offer a vital tool for opening a broad—but informed—guidance to the web.

The Argus Clearinghouse: The Internet's Premier Research Library
http://www.clearinghouse.net

This outstanding site is a spin-off from the University of Michigan's School of Information Science and is currently headed by a graduate of the program, Louis Rosenfeld. The Clearinghouse offers over 400 hypertext guides that cover a very broad array of topics and includes virtually every academic discipline. The guides are frequently updated so as to maintain currency, and there is a steady submission of new guides.

The site is organized around thirteen major subject categories starting with *Arts & Humanities* and concluding with *Social Sciences & Social Issues*. Guides are submitted by librarians, academics, and independent scholars and researchers and then rated by the Clearinghouse staff. Guides are ranked in ascending order from one to five, and criteria include focus, comprehensiveness, usability, design, organization, etc. Clearly, some guides are better than others, but on the whole the quality is uniformly high. The Clearinghouse's main page offers a search engine managed by a loose keyword index. For instance, "history" as a search term retrieves forty-eight separate guides. The guides cover a broad array of historical periods, geographical regions, and historical subdisciplines. Moreover, most of the individual guides feature their own search engines. Like "history", the major disciplines, offer a good number of guides to choose from. The Clearinghouse encompasses a great deal of diverse information, yet at the same time is easy to understand and use.

MAGELLAN
INTERNET GUIDE

http://www.mckinley.com

This site is the product of the McKinley Group, which, in turn, is an affiliate of Excite Inc. Magellan pioneered attempts at bringing order to the web by presenting descriptions and reviews of individual sites. Magellan offers three different search options. One can search either the entire web, restrict searches to reviewed sites or even more narrowly restrict searches to what are dubbed greenlight sites. The greenlight sites are aimed at protecting kids. The reviewed sites are ranked from one to four stars, and the text is generally limited to one to three sentences and tends to be more descriptive than evaluative. Overall, the site is less geared toward academics than entertainment popular *Crafts* or *People Pages: A to Z* and *Love Stories* do not exactly inspire confidence for those seeking research material. On the other hand, one should not dismiss Magellan too lightly in that the database includes numerous outstanding academic sites. There are several different ways to search Magellan. The first, and most obvious, is to click on the button for reviewed sites on the main page and then simply type in a search term. Generally, this will retrieve a large number of items that the search engine attempts to sort according to relevancy, although the accuracy is sometimes questionable. To make the list more manageable, one can click on the "topic" line, which is listed just below the title of the site and which offers a focused subject heading, and retrieve a list of what are specified as "featured reviews." Sites are ranked, usually not over a dozen, in descending order from four star sites to two star sites.

The surest means of arriving at academic sites with "featured reviews" is to click on the category *Education: Universities, K-12* on Magellan's main page. A number of options are available from the *Education* page, of which the most relevant for our purposes is the category *Field of Study*. There are choices for either *Arts & Humanities* or *Social Science* fields, and from each of these categories one can focus on individual disciplines and sub-disciplines. For the sciences, there is a separate button on the Magellan main page. Magellan offers a number of different ways to search and at first view is misleadingly simple. However, patience and a little investigation of how Magellan organizes information can pay off with nice dividends.

The WWW Virtual Library

WWW Virtual Library
http://vlib.org/Overview.html

This site has impeccable academic credentials. It is an offshoot of the World Wide Web Consortium (W3C) hosted by the Massachusetts Institute of Technology. The management and membership of W3C is truly international and includes some of the best minds working in the field of electronic communications. However, the Virtual Library represents only a small part of W3C activity.

On the main page subject guides are arranged alphabetically starting with *Aboriginal Studies* and concluding with *Zoos*. The vast majority of the guides are resolutely academic in tone, although one can also find occasional oddities such as guides to *Paranormal Phenomena* and *Roadkill*. The list editors request submission of guides from volunteers, and the result is a very eclectic coverage of the academic terrain. For instance, there are guides addressed to *Sumeria*, *Mycology*, and *Cognitive Science*, yet not one devoted to a field as fundamental as psychology. In short, the coverage is broad but spotty. Moreover, a number of the guides sampled have not been well maintained or updated such that there are a number of dead links. On the other hand, there are a number of outstanding guides that are not listed elsewhere. The simple alphabetic arrangement of the subject guides makes the Virtual Library easy to browse. Another nice feature of the Virtual Library is that the main page includes links to other meta-subject indexes.

Galaxy: The professional's guide to a world of information
http://www.einet.net/galaxy.html

This site is generously sponsored by America's Health Network. There are several different ways to search Galaxy. The main page features a search engine that allows either simple keyword or advanced searching. The latter enables one to search the entire text of a web site or restrict the search to just title words or linking text within sites. One can truncate, employ boolean operators, and other sophisticated searching techniques. Search results are sorted by relevancy, but most importantly Galaxy furnishes a good deal of additional information. For instance, individual sites are given a descriptive profile drawn from an excerpt from the site's main page, and there is even a count of the most frequent keywords appearing on the site. Furthermore, individual sites are mapped to Galaxy subject heading that, in turn, lead to sites addressing similar materials or concerns.

The second way to search Galaxy is through its own assigned subject headings. The main page represents nine broad subject fields, including *Business and Commerce, Humanities, Science,* etc. Clicking on any one of these categories opens an alphabetical directory of fields representing virtually every academic discipline. In turn, clicking on an individual discipline furnishes a broad but focused survey of web resources in the field. Most major disciplines, like psychology, will feature links representing principal subdivisions within the field such as clinical psychology, experimental psychology, social psychology, etc. In short, Galaxy subject headings provide a neat and orderly articulation of the academic universe.

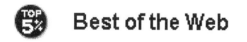 # Best of the Web

---

http://point.lycos.com

Best of the Web is an offshoot of the popular Lycos search engine and as the title suggests limits itself to what the editors consider the top 5% of all web sites. There are over 10,000 sites reviewed, as opposed to the thirty million plus in the entire Lycos database. Sites are judged by three criteria: content, presentation, and what the editors dub overall experience. Each site is given a number between one and fifty for each of the criteria. It is easy to note from the main page that the site is more oriented toward popular as opposed to academic tastes. For instance, among the eighteen broad headings posted on the main page one will find *Fashion, Lifestyle, Shopping, Entertainment,* and the like. On the other hand, one will find many academic and research oriented sites under the headings *Arts and Humanities* and *Science and Technology.*

There are a number of different ways to search the database. Each method yields very different results, so it is important to take some care in deciding upon a search strategy. First, one can click on *Science and Technology* and then select an individual discipline. The result is a short list of sites, usually not over twenty, that are sorted by their numerical ranking. The problem with this search is the very limited number of featured sites and, in certain cases, the poor fit between the discipline selected and the sites listed. For instance, who would imagine that the number one ranked site for sociology would be *Humanities Hub.* In sum, I would only recommend this method of searching the database to those looking for a quick and dirty search.

Second, one can simply type in a discipline or topic on the search bar located at the top of the main page. This yields a simple keyword search and often over a hundred hits. There is no evident ranking of the sites, but there are short and helpful descriptions of the sites. Moreover, there are bars attached to each of the sites which enable one to automatically map the search term to what is specified as *Sites by Subject.* Although the operation is not obvious on the surface, the search results are much more precise. This I consider the preferred method of getting the most out of the database.

Third, one can achieve much the same result by clicking on *Custom Search* on the main page. Here, one is presented with a more advanced search engine that is not limited to key words. There are a number of options available, including restricting searches to *Sites by Subject* and allowing a differential degree of match to subject such as loose, good, strong, etc. To reiterate, this is an interesting and rich site, yet to get the most out of it requires some time and patience.

---

http://www.ipl.org

This site is hosted by the University of Michigan's School of Information Science. A quick glance at the site's main page headings, like *Youth, Teen,* and *MOO,* could easily lead to the conclusion that the primary orientation is toward a younger clientele. However, this is not necessarily the case.

Clicking on the bar marked *Reference* summons a group of sites categorized by broad headings like *Social Sciences*, or *Sciences & Technology*. Clicking on any one of these categories yields a list of disciplines, and then under each discipline are listed fifteen or so prominent sites devoted to that area. Individual sites, in turn, are furnished with a brief report, and uniform subject headings are assigned, along with an author or contact address. One very nice feature is that if a site is assigned multiple subject headings then a linkage is established to the alternative subjects. Although there are no hard criteria by which sites are included, it is clear that sites have been carefully selected in terms of furnishing a broad overview of a particular field.

The *Reference Center* also boasts an online reference desk. However, patrons are reminded that reference questions should be precisely worded and to the point, and they should also keep in mind that it may take a few days to respond. Finally, buried under the heading *Teen* on the main page, one finds the heading *Research and Writing Guide*. Located here is a useful compendium of information and advice on how to construct research papers and reports. The guidance offered is not merely relevant to teens. In this regard, the Internet Public Library caters to a larger audience than might appear at first glance.

EDUCATION index™

http://www.educationindex.com

This site is sponsored by College View, a software producer out of Cincinnati. Like the Internet Public Library, initial impressions are misleading. The main page features a critter called the "Web Weasel," which does not sound very promising. However, exploration of the sites grouped under the *SUBJECT* button indicates the site holds a good deal of promise.

All in all there are fifty-five disciplines represented, ranging from *Agriculture* to *Women's Studies*. Although there is no attempt

to rank individual sites, each of the featured sites has a brief annotation explaining its particular virtues. Moreover, it is clear that the editors have attempted to offer a balanced view of the types of questions and research that are characteristic of each discipline. The Education Index may not be the most sophisticated meta-subject guide, but it nonetheless offers a good deal of promise for those just getting their feet wet.

Infomine: Scholarly Internet Resource Collections

http://infomine.ucr.edu

This site, sponsored by the University of California, Riverside, is an outstanding example of the growing number of academic subject guides that one can find on university library homepages. Infomine boasts 14,000 plus sites geared specifically toward academic and research interests. It is readily apparent that sites have been carefully selected with a primary emphasis on content. Equally impressive is the site's clear and systematic organization and depth of indexing and cross-referencing.

Infomine is divided into ten broad subject categories, starting with *Biological, Agricultural & Medical Sciences* and concluding with *Visual & Performing Arts*. Clicking on a subject category calls up a page that allows a number of different search options. First, an internal search engine allows one to search by subject, title or keyword, or all three. Second, there are several different methods of browsing the database. The bar for *Table of Contents* lists subject areas alphabetically and then the titles of individual sites featured under each subject area. The bar for *Subject* simply lists the number of sites attached to a subject, such as *History (93)*.

In addition, there are bars for browsing by *Keyword* and *Title*. Finally, each site retrieved by clicking on a subject category is furnished not only with a solid description of its contents, but also a bar that opens the door to the exploration of related resources. Clicking on the bar yields an elaborate record that provides direct cross references to related subjects and keywords. In addition, the record has a more complete description of the site and the academic fields to which it applies. A complete record may be three pages long,which affords an unparalleled level of indexing.

As mentioned above, a growing number of university libraries and academic departments are now posting their own subject guides on the web, and even though they may not be as complete and as detailed as Infomine there are many good guides available. Moreover, we can anticipate, as the web becomes an increasingly regular feature of the academic landscape, that subject guides and individual sites will become more and more sophisticated and information rich. In this regard, Infomine offers an ideal model. For a slightly different angle on web subject access one might also investigate Rice University's web subject guides at **http://riceinfo.rice.edu/Fondren/ Netguides/** or Louisiana State University Libraries so-called webliographies at **http://www.lib.lsu.edu/weblio. html**.

Social Science

There are a number of good guides that focus on the entire range of the social sciences, as opposed to individual disciplines. Some of these guidesare stronger in certain areas of the social sciences than others, but all of the sites featured in this chapter are notable for their multidisciplinary outlook. If one's primary orientation is toward the social sciences, the sites below offer a focused view of the web and at the same time grant a broad range of choices.

Social Sciences Virtual Library

http://www.clas.ufl.edu/users/ gthursby/socsci/

This site is maintained by Professor Gene Thursby, Religion Studies, University of Florida. In effect, the site represents a subset of the much larger WWW Virtual Library discussed in the previous chapter. The main page presents a *Table of Contents,* which has an alphabetical listing of social science sites and also contains a number of directories to relevant electronic journals, data archives, and the like. However, the richest category featured on the main page is *WWW Resources by Subject.* Here, Professor Thursby divvies up the social sciences into thirteen major fields starting with *Anthropology* and concluding with what he calls *Systems—Artificial and Natural.*

Each headings is broken down into fields and subdisciplines with a single site attached. In other words, there is not a lot of choice involved. On the other hand, the individual guides are of uniform high quality. Professor Thursby has an inclusive and expansive vision of the social sciences. Generally, one would not find disciplines like dance or theater and drama listed as a social science, but this is a minor caveat. The distinguishing trait of the Social Sciences WWW Virtual Library is the breadth of the subjects covered, combined with a neat and concise package. A comparable general resource also worth exploring is Professor Craig McKie's **Research Resources for the Social Sciences** at **http://www.socsciresearch. com**.

Data on the Internet

http://odwin.ucsd.edu/jj/idata/

This marvelous site is located at the University of San Diego. The emphasis here is on quantitative and statistical data, which is the backbone of much social science research. There are 750 plus sites represented from all over the world. Most of the sites are government related, but not exclusively so. The type of data one finds here pertains to education, elections, population, economics, etc., or virtually any aspect of human social activity that can be counted.

There are a number of different ways to search the site. At the top of the main page is a search engine that searches the titles, table of contents, and descriptions of all 750 links. Use the search engine with caution. For instance, if one inputs a very general term like education, the result will be an overwhelming number of sites, many of which will be of questionable relevance. The one real weakness of the database is that individual sites are not assigned subject headings proper. On the other hand, just below the search engine, there are bars distinguishing different types of data sites, such that *Data Archives* is a separate category from *Searchable Catalogs of Data.* Under each of the bars, sites are listed in simple alphabetical order. A good deal of browsing may be involved before one finds a database or link of interest. Each site is given a solid and precise description of its contents, and many of the sites are furnished with their own internal search engine linked to the University of San Diego. This is an impressive feature, indeed. The one thing to keep in mind when employing Data on the Internet is that one might have to do a good deal of exploration and digging to fully exploit the richness of the site.

Inter-University Consortium for Political and Social Research (ICPSR)
http://www.icpsr.umich.edu

This enormous site, housed at the University of Michigan, boasts the world's largest archive of computerized social science data. One can find literally thousands of data sets from all over the world. One should understand from the outset that ICPSR is oriented toward advanced empricial research in the social sciences. On the surface, however, the archive appears easily accessible and features a browsable table of contents. There are eighteen subjects listed alphabetically starting with *Census Enumerations* and concluding with *Social Institutions*. There is also a button allowing a search of the entire archive by keyword, title or primary investigator. Retrieval by keyword can be a bit overwhelming unless one has a very precise title or topic in mind. On these grounds, the subject oriented table of contents is recommended.

Clicking on one of the subject categories offers first a choice of national studies, and this is followed by an alphabetized list of titles. Each title is furnished with an abstract and data buttons. Clicking on abstracts yields a highly detailed description of the breadth and scope of the data. Here, one also finds information about data type, source, format, methodology, funding source, etc. Selecting a data button retrieves a list of individual files comprising the data set, which can range from a single file to hundreds. One can also download data in com-pressed or uncompressed format, but only if one is affiliated with an ICPSR member insti-tution. In short, one cannot retrieve data to the screen immediately.

ICPSR is not designed to run down discrete facts, but rather is aimed at the researcher requiring a mass of data in order to manipulate it. The issue of authorized use in not as problematic as might appear on the surface in that many universities large and small are affiliated with ICPSR. The more trying problem is possessing the technical expertise, which one might well find in an upper division undergraduate, to take advantage of the materials housed at ICPSR. Even if one is not primarily interested in downloading data it is an engaging exercise to simply browse and explore the immense range of ICPSR subjects and titles.

SOSIG: Social Science Information Gateway
http://www.esrc.bris.ac.uk

This site was developed by the Institute for Research and Learning Technology at the University of Bristol. SOSIG includes links to thousands of high quality resources with the value-added benefit of systematic cataloging and cross-referencing. The site is maintained in exemplary fashion and is easy to navigate.

There are several ways to search SOSIG. There is a search engine that scans the entire site and retrieves any matching word from the description or the subject heading assigned to a specific site. Owing to the detailed cataloging and description of the site, search results tend to be very precise. One can also search a specific subject or discipline by clicking on either *Worldwide Social Science Resources* or *UK-based Social Science Resources*. The latter is naturally more intensively focused on the U.K. Twenty-five social science disciplines are listed in alphabetic order, starting with *Accountancy* and concluding with *Statistics*. Each discipline, in turn, alphabetically lists fifty to more than a hundred recommended sites. It might take a spell to plow through the sites listed by discipline. On the other hand, there is a good deal to be said in favor of the browsability of the sites listed, and in any case the numbers are not overwhelming. To reiterate, SOSIG is notable for the great care dedicated to organizing the site so as to maximize its utility.

Research Methods Knowledge Base

http://trochim.human.cornell.edu/ kb/index.htm

This ingenious site is the creation of Professor Bill Trochim, Department of Human Service Studies, Cornell University. Professor Trochim has dabbled extensively in employing the Internet as a teaching tool. One of the fruits of his labor, *Knowledge Base*, is the installation of a full online textbook for an introductory course in social science research methods.

The text is more personal and idiosyncratic than most introductory methods texts, but that is all to the good. One is treated to a full exposition on how a distinguished social researcher views his craft. We also encourage a visit to Professor Trochim's personal homepage where he has placed documents and links to a wide variety of sites focused on social research methods. The homepage is located at, **http:// trochim.human.cornell.edu**.

Anthropology and Archaeology

Anthropology and archaeology are among the most interdisciplinary academic fields. One generally conceives of them as studying past or primitive cultures and civilizations, but this is not necessarily the case. One can find ethnographers and cultural linguists exploring contemporary modern urban settings, and there are industrial archaeologists who unearth the recent past. In the broadest terms, one can argue that these disciplines examine human behavior in its cultural and social dimensions, but one can also find anthropologists studying social organization and behavior amongst primates, wolves and crows. In short, anthropology, of which archaeology is actually a subdiscipline, covers a lot of territory. The field of anthropology is divided into several major subdisciplines each of which has its own distinctive methodology and research traditions. First there is the previously mentioned field of archaeology, and then there is social or cultural anthroplogy, physical or biological anthropology, and linguistic anthropology. At the outset this chapter looks at the field in a comprehensive way and then focuses on the individual subdisciplines.

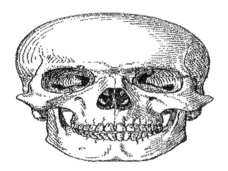

Anthropology Resources on the Internet

http://home.worldnet.fr/clist/Anthro/index.html

This enormous site was originally assembled by the part-time archaeologist and devoted web explorer allen h. lutins, and is presently maintained by bernard-olivier clist (both of whom prefer not to capitalize their names). The site lists general anthropological servers, yet also has extensive sections dedicated to each of the major subdisciplines, such that there are separate headings for cultural anthropology, archaeology, physical anthropology, and linguistic anthropology. In addition, there are separate headings for museums, academic departments, commercial sites, etc. Anthropology Resources is frequently updated, and the arrangement of the linkages is very simple and easy to follow.

Individual sites are listed alphabetically under each heading or subdiscipline, and there is often a very brief description of the content and focus of the site. If one wants to browse a broad range of anthropological web sites then Anthropology Resources is the perfect launching point.

Anthropology in the News

http://www.tamu.edu/anthropology/news.html

This very useful site is maintained by Professor David Carlson, Anthropology Department, Texas A&M University. The site consists of links to full-text articles dealing with anthropology or anthropological related issues. The articles are culled from a number of different online news sources including the *New York Times*, *Washington Post*, Associated Press, ABC, etc.

Even though the articles tend to be brief, and are not the kind of thing one would find in scholarly journals, they are nonetheless high quality and interesting works. Professor Carlson updates the site on an almost daily basis. Under the title *Breaking News*, articles are listed according to their currency. There are also separate listings for *Archaeology*, *Bioanthropology*, *Social/Cultural*, and *Linguistics*. For those interested in up-to-date information on the kinds of work and research that involve anthropology this is a highly recommended resource.

ArchNet: World Wide Virtual Library for Archaeology
http://archnet.uconn.edu

This extremely well organized and impressive site was assembled by Thomas Plunkett and Jonathan Lizee for the Anthropology Department, University of Connecticut. One can browse ArchNet through a series of menus, or one can employ a search engine for more focused questions. The search engine can be very effective for highly specific queries but is less helpful for general exploration of ArchNet. For the latter it is recommended to use either the table of contents or buttons located on the homepage.

The site is divided into a number of different categories, the two most important of which are *Regional View* and *Subject Areas*. Under *Regional View*, the globe is divided into eight geographical regions each of which includes an alphabetic listing of nations and regions within that geographic sector. For instance, if one clicks on Europe, one will find seventeen separate sites listed under France. On the other hand, looking under *Subject Areas* retrieves fourteen separate categories or subdisciplines such as *Archaeometry, Ceramics, Geo-Archaeology, Lithics*, and the like. One will also find here *Educational Resources,* listing a number of different college course syllabi and outlines. There is also a selection of reference works, such as a *Glossary of Archaeological Terms*. Another subject area of great interest is *Site Files and Tours*, which focuses on individual archaeological digs all over the world. In addition, there are buttons on the homepage for archaeologically oriented *Academic Departments, Journals & Publishers* and a marvelous collection of *Museums*. If one's

interest is archaeology , this is clearly the site to go with.

http://www.pro-am.com/origins

This site, maintained by Jeff Rix, is devoted to human evolution, paleoanthropology, physical anthropology and, more specifically, prehistoric man. At first glance the homepage appears a bit busy and cluttered looking, but it is not difficult to navigate. The meat of the site is positioned on the left side of the page, under *Main Menu.* Located here are five topical categories, including links to newsgroups and listservs, and a nice list of current books pertaining to human evolution.

The most substantive links, however, are listed under the headings of *Research Center* and *Origins Links*. The former presents a chronology of human evolution featuring separate links to *Australophithecus, Homo hablis, Cro-Magnon*, etc. The articles tend to be short but illustrate well the complexity of human evolution. Also located here are full-text versions of Charles Darwin's *Voyage of the Beagle* and *Origins of the Species*. There is a very broad array of material listed under the *Origins Links* heading. It is divided into ten topical subheadings, including *Information Sites, Merchandise, Museums & Labs, Organizations*, etc. This is kind of an odd mix, yet if one is in the market for a scientifically accurate model of a neanderthal skull than one has found just the place. Despite the occasional curiosity there are a good number of relevant and high-quality links illustrating the scientific literature and course of human evolution.

The Centre for Social Anthropology and Computing: CSAC's Ethnographics Gallery
http://lucy.ukc.ac.uk/index.html

This rich site, oriented toward social/cultural anthropology, comes to us from the University of Kent at Canterbury. The layout is elaborate, and it is not immediately apparent the vast stores of information located here. The homepage presents a number of buttons and bars offering diverse search options.

First, there is a button for a search engine that scans the entire site. There is no problem with retrieving items, yet there is some question about their relevancy. Perhaps the best use for the search engine is to quickly locate items that one knows are available at the site. Second, under the button entitled *Research* are located a distinguished array of full-text articles undertaken by CSAC researchers. A sampling of the titles include, *Making Tradition in the Cook Islands*, *Vims: The Virtual Institute of Mambila Studies*, *Impressions of Sienna: A Pictorial Guide through Contrada Life*, and the extraordinary field notes and reminiscences of Paul Sterling *45 Years in a Turkish Village*. These articles and projects provide a unique online insight into the range and breadth of questions posed by social/cultural anthropologists. Third, there is a button for *Resources*, which includes a hodgepodge of homegrown items and external links. Located here are book reviews, bibliographies,etc. Particularly notable is their own electronic journal *CSAC Studies in Anthropology*, and external links to *Anthropology Exhibits on the WWW*. Fourth, clicking on the button entitled *Links* retrieves an interesting and well chosen set of external links to anthropological related sites.

Finally, toward the tail end of the homepage are three buttons—*Search Bibliographies*, *Search Theses*, and *RAI*. The first two buttons represent databases of anthropology related bibliographies and U.K. theses that would be of limited interest to the undergraduate. However, *RAI* represents the *Anthropological Index Online*, published by the Royal Anthropological Institute. This is a very powerful periodical index that covers the literature from 1965 to the present. Hundreds of journals from all corners of the globe are indexed . The index allows one to search either by keyword, subject heading, author, title, or journal. In short, this is a marvelous tool for locating anthropological literature. Generally, one is not allowed free access to professional indexes of this sort. *RAI* is only one of the many fine features of the CSAC site. It bears keeping in mind that although it requires some effort, the CSAC affords substantial dividends to the determined explorer.

ETHNOLOGUE

http://www.sil.org/ethnologue/

This fascinating site, sponsored by the Summer Institute of Linguistics at Dallas, offers an online version of the thirteenth edition of the text, *Ethnologue: Languages of the World*. Barbara Grimes, the chief editor of the enterprise, and her consulting editors, Richard Pittman and Joseph Grimes, have endeavored to assemble a comprehensive list of global languages.

The print version alone weighs in at a massive 966 pages. No one can say with absolute precision how many languages there are in the world today, but when one adds up all the names of known languages and their alternate names the total exceeds a stunning 39,304. The volume also features a solid preface and introduction. The essential organization of the text is geographic.

The initial page opens with a bar representing each of the continents. Clicking on a continent retrieves a list of nations. Clicking on a nation, in turn, retrieves a document listing the languages spoken in that particular nation. At the head of each of these national profiles there is a brief breakdown of national ethnic composition. Each language listed is furnished with a brief but precise description. Details included are the number of speakers of the language, the geographic range of the language, distinctive dialects and familial relations with other languages, variant names of the language, etc. For instance, if one selects the profile of the languages spoken in the United States, one is presented with a twenty-five page document listing 213 languages. Most of the languages listed are Native American, and many of those are on the verge of extinction. However, one will also find all kinds of regional English, French, and Spanish dialects, and distinctive languages like *Amerax* which is a neo-Muslim tongue developed in American prisons. Cumulatively, what emerges is a mosaic of tremendous diversity and complexity.

One is not restricted to merely a geographic setting in that there is also a keyword search engine that scans the entire database. For instance, if one employs "French" as a query, one retrieves a 284 item list detailing, across the globe, where french or some dialect is spoken or taught. In addition, the site includes maps of the continents, a massive bibliography, and two separate indexes, the *Ethnologue Language Name Index* and the *Ethnologue Language Family Index*. The former offers a simple alphabetized list of languages, and the latter groups languages by family and affiliation. There are also a number of external links scattered throughout the database. Ethnologue is under constant revision, with a new text planned every four years. This is a model academic resource available via the web.

National Museum of the American Indian

http://www.si.edu/organiza/ museums/amerind/start.htm

This site showcases one of the many branches of the Smithsonian. Anthropologists are, of course, interested in cultures all over the world, but there has been a particular devotion to studies of the American Indian. The site not only furnishes information about the museum and its vast collection of over a million items, but also chronicles a continuous series of on-line exhibitions.

For instance, an attractive exhibition entitled *Woven by the Grandmothers: Nineteenth-Century Navajo Textiles from the National Museum of the American Indian,* showcases the museum's unique collection of Navajo blankets. There are many other cultural treasures on display at the National Museum of the American Indian.

If one requires more specific information about individual tribes, then I recommend the very fine page assembled by Lisa Mitten at the University of Pittsburgh, **Native American Sites** located at **http://www.pitt.edu/~lmitten/ indians.html**. One can also profitably peruse Anita Cohen-Williams' site at the University of Arizona, **Anthropology and American Indian Sites on the Internet** located at **http://dizzy. library.arizona.edu/users/jlcox/first.html**.

Business

Business does not fit neatly as a social science, and at most universities, the business college stands as a separate entity from the rest of the social sciences. On the other hand, business as an academic discipline draws heavily from other social sciences, such as economics, sociology, psychology, demography, etc., and like the other social sciences its explanatory power is founded on rigorous empirical enquiry. Another obvious feature of business is that it is profit oriented and that business leaders and entrepreneurs are extremely pragmatic in achieving that goal. In practice the aim of accumulating capital overwhelms the social science goal of affording a neat explanation.

In any case, the focus here is business as an academic discipline as opposed to business as an activity, hence the rationale for lumping business with the social sciences. Like most other academic disciplines business is divided into a number of distinctive subdisciplines. Business' field of activities is so large that we can not cover all of the subfields, but will focus on the major subdisciplines: accounting, advertising and marketing, finance, management, and human resources. One thing that must be made clear is that there is a staggering number or academic and commercial sites devoted to business. The search engine Yahoo at present includes more than 200,000 corporate and company homepages. This chapter focuses on a few outstanding sites so as to convey the breadth of activity and materials available for business research on the web.

Internet Sources for
U.S. Corporate, Industrial, and Economic Information

Internet Sources for U.S. Corporate, Industrial, and Economic Information
http://libweb.uncc.edu/ref-bus/ buselec.htm

The title may be a little unwieldy, but this is an excellent resource for general business information. The site is the creation of Jeanne Welch, Business Librarian, J. Murrey Atkins Library, University of North Carolina at Charlotte. The layout is simple and easy to understand. At the top of the page, there is a table of contents that translates into nine major topical categories including *Business News*, *Company Information*, *Industry Information*, *Jobs, Careers & Labor*, *Legal Resources*, *Other Business Meta-Pages*, *Stocks, Bonds & Mutual Funds*, *US Economic Data*, and *Regional/State/ Local Economic Data*.

Each of these categories generally represents dozens of sites, yet the list is not so extensive as to be overwhelming. Although the individual sites are not annotated, it is clear they have been carefully selected. If one is seeking a guide to all aspects of business resources on the web, then Ms. Welch's site is an ideal launching point. A slightly fuller page is available at Cornell University **BII-Business Internet Index** at **http://www.library.cornell. edu/jgsm/library/BII/BII.html**.

Access Business Online's Daily

Business Newspaper
http://www.clickit.com/touch/home. htm

This is a huge site devoted to current business news. The newspaper has a very professional look and feel and is updated three times daily. Information is drawn from a wide array of news and wire services, and there is also an in-house editorial staff. At first glance, the homepage is a bit overwhelming, in that there is an explosion of buttons and bars designating different topics and sectors within the site. However, it is assumed that the majority of readers have very specific interests so that if they are involved, for instance, in liquidations, they can jump right to the topic, rather than leaf through the entire paper. In addition, there are over 40,000 links, so that the site requires a good deal of articulation in order to make it manageable.

The paper is certainly geared more toward professional people, rather than students and academics, but it does provide a unique insight into the day-to-day workings of business' movers and shakers.

Hoover's Online: The Source for Company Information

http://www.hoovers.com

Hoover's is a prominent publisher of business reference sources. One of the most frequent assignments for business students is researching company profiles, and Hoover's speciality is compiling up-to-date company profiles. One might refer to this as a two-tiered site, in that there is a lot of information here for free, yet there is also information for sale.

Hoover's furnishes free information for over 10,000 of the world's largest public and private enterprises, but one can also subscribe to a service that provides much more detailed information for 2,700 companies. Hoover's is searchable either by company name or ticker symbol. A company profile generally consists of a short narrative of the company's primary business and then lists addresses and numbers for the company, a web address, the officers of the company, baseline annual sales and earnings figures, number of employees, and ticker symbol. In addition, for publicly traded corporations, there are valuable links to the company's stock performance and a very detailed financial report filed with the Securities and Exchange Commission (more on this later). Finally, there are links to news services that post any recent press releases about the company in question. In short, Hoover's is a powerful tool for researching company profiles.

http://www.wsrn.com

This huge site with over 250,000 links offers another way to research companies with an especial focus on stocks, investments and financial information. The site is divided into eight separate categories, the most important of which is devoted to company research.

Over 17,000 publicly traded companies are listed in the database. The search engine is quick and simple and can search either by company name or ticker symbol. What is astonishing is the amount of detailed information the search retrieves. Although there is not, like in Hoover's, a broad summary of a company, there are dozens of links to sources that graph and chart a company's performance. For those who play the stock market, or those assigned to track a stock, Wall Street Research Net is unrivaled in the multidimensional scope of the information it provides.

In addition, the site furnishes valuable links to domestic and foreign stock exchanges, business news from a number of wire services, a directory of web accessible investment brokers, and an impressive searchable database of mutual funds. For a somewhat broader view of finance that goes beyond company profiles and stock performance, try **OSU Virtual Finance Library** sponsored by Ohio State University's Department of Finance, **http://www.cob.ohio-state.edu/fin/cerns.htm**.

A Business Researcher's Interests

A Business Researcher's Interests: BizTech Research Library & Searchable Knowledge Map

http://www.brint.com/interest.html

This site was developed by the management consultant and Internet guru Yogesh Malhotra. Although one can find a bit of everything here with regard to business, the primary focus is on management and technology issues.

The site is vast in terms of size and scope, and at first glance, the page appears busy and difficult to navigate. A search engine is available on the initial page, but for the first time user the best way to explore the site is through the table of contents. The latter is very well articulated and runs a full seven pages in length. For instance, under the heading *Management* there are separate sections dedicated to *Business Process Reengineering & Innovation, Knowledge Management & Organizational Learning, Virtual Corporations & Outsourcing, Complex Systems & Chaos Theory*, etc. Each one of the sections, in turn, is divided among a number of different subheadings, which offer a broad array of material including full-text papers, journal articles, case studies and tools, and hundreds of links to other resources. If one is looking for more specialized areas of management try, **Human Resource Management Resources on the Internet** at **http://www.nbs.ntu.ac.uk/staff/lyerj//hrm_link.htm** or the impressive **TWIGG's Operations Management Index** at **http://members.tripod.com/~wwwtomi/index.html**.

Accounting Resources on the Internet

http://www.rutgers.edu/ Accounting/raw/internet/

This comprehensive site is maintained by Dr. Alex Kogan, Rutgers University Accounting Research Center. As one might expect from an accountant, this is an extremely well organized site. The homepage features seventeen bars representing different categories of information. Each bar then alphabetically lists a number of relevant sites. For instance, several bars are devoted to specialist areas within accounting such, as *Finance, Taxation, Audit & Law, Government*, etc. Other bars target more general resources like accounting firms, assoc-

iations, e-journals, standards, publishers and other related accounting sites. The ease of navigating Accounting Resources on the Internet testifies to the site's superior organization.

Advertising World

Advertising World: The Ultimate Marketing Communications Directory
http://advweb.cocomm.utexas.edu/ world

This site arrives courtesy of the Department of Advertising, University of Texas. The creators of the site have scoured the web compiling a rich compendium of advertising and marketing venues. The index to Advertising World covers an impressive seventy-two major categories, starting with *Account Planning* and concluding with *Web Site Promotion*.

One gains a good idea of the comprehensiveness of the site by simply enumerating some of the categories represented: *Advertising Agencies, Consultants & Experts, Consumer Psychology, Creative Services, Direct Marketing, History & Museums* (specifically devoted to advertising), *Market Research, Political Advertising, Sales Promotions, Targeting & Segmentation* (focus on various ethnic cultures and lifestyles) and *Unconventional Media*. Most of the links are to companies that furnish services in these varied areas, but one will also find original papers, bibliographies, and other materials. If one desires a more international perspective on marketing and advertising, try Erik-Jan Gelink's site from the Netherlands, **EJ's Marketing and Sales HomePage** at **http://www.xs4all.nl/~egelink/**.

International Business Resources On The WWW

IBR: International Business Resources on the WWW
http://ciber.bus.mus.edu/busres.htm

This site is maintained by the Center for International Business Education and Research, Michigan State University. As the economy becomes increasingly globalized there is more and more need for a site that profiles international business activity and opportunities for trade and investment.

The site is divided into nineteen distinct sections, each of which lists a variety of relevant links. Of especial value here are the concise abstracts attached to each of the links. Categories include such topics as news and journals, trade information and leads, statistical data, company directories, foreign and domestic government resources, etc. However, at the heart of the enterprise are the sections headed *Regional or Country Specific Information*. Each of these sections devoted to individual nations boasts a broad array of commercial, associational, and government resources. Many of the profiles of individual nations furnish step-by-step guides on how to establish trade relations. There is also solid information on what pitfalls to avoid and what nations and economies it is best to steer clear of.

In addition to the regional focus there is a valuable section entitled, *Various Utilities and Useful Information*. Here, one finds practical tools for conducting international business like currency convertors, a world clock, airlines and flight information, shipping guides, etc. In short, International Business Resources on the WWW offers a wealth of information to student, teacher and seasoned practitioner.

http://www.edgar-online.com/brand/ university

EDGAR was purposefully saved for the last. It was one of the first powerful databases to emerge on the web and helped demonstrate the potential of the web for information access. EDGAR is an acronym for Electronic Data

Gathering Analysis and Retrieval System and first operated as an expensive electronic subscription service with very limited access. The Securities and Exchange Commission was the original title-holder to the data, and with the advent of the Internet it was decided that the SEC itself would take over complete control of EDGAR and furnish free access via the web, gopher, ftp, etc. One might say that the transformation of EDGAR from an exclusive fee-paying service to a free service attests to the democratizing influence of the web.

In any case, EDGAR houses the electronic depositions that all publicly traded companies are required to file with the SEC. Formerly, the collection was somewhat spotty, in that companies were not required to file electronically. However, since May 6, 1996, all public companies have been required to file electronically. There are many types of forms that companies are required to file with the SEC, but generally the most userful are the 10q and 10k forms. The 10q form is the quarterly financial report, and it essentially offers a quick baseline snapshot of performance. The 10k form is the annual report that companies must file within sixty days of the end of their fiscal year. This is an infinitely more substantial and detailed examination of virtually anything that can be quantified regarding a companies total operation. It is not unusual for a major corporation's 10k to take up 1/2 meg of disc space, or eight to one hundred pages of text. This is a tremendous amount of information that furnishes an in depth view into a companies standing and performance.

There are several different models of EDGAR available on the web, yet I chose a commercially developed version because it furnishes a superior search form that is both flexible and easy to use. One can search by either company name, or ticker number. Searches can also be limited by form type (10k, 10q, etc.), and filing date. This is a superior tool for research on public companies. If one is curious to see the SEC's original version of EDGAR it is located at **http://www.sec.gov/ edgarhp.htm**.

Communication Studies

Communications is a relatively youthful but vigorously expanding discipline that is attracting more and more students as a major. The field is devoted to addressing the entire scope of human communication and interaction. It is owing to this lofty inclusiveness that communication studies often appears to lack any central focus.

What can be said with certainty is that communications is a multidisciplinary field encompassing both the social sciences and the humanities. Research can range from highly rigorous and quantitative studies of mass media and public opinion to the most *au courant* critical/cultural theory. In this environment it is thus typical for communication departments to address issues as widely scattered as classical rhetoric, speech and persuasion, theoretical and applied aspects of broadcasting, film studies, journalism, mass media studies, small group communication, public relations and advertising, and a host of other related subdisciplines. Communication researchers are especially interested in exploring new communication technologies, like the Internet. As a consequence, there are a number of outstanding web sites devoted to showcasing various aspects of the dynamic field of communication studies.

is certainly not parochial. The site is constructed around a broad array of subject headings, including *Gender and Ethnicity, Advertising, Media Education, Textual Analysis, TV & Radio, Pop Music/Youth, Active Interpretation, Visual Image, Film Studies, Media Influence, News Media*, etc. Each of these headings, in turn, is divided into a number of subheading. For example, located under the general heading *Textual Analysis* are separate categories for different types of analysis such as, *Semiotics, Genre Theory, Intertextuality, Narratology, Content Analysis, Discourse Analysis* and *Rhetorical Analysis*. The categories then furnish links to relevant essays, discussions and treatments of the type of analysis in question. In short, the material is effectively organized.

Moreover, in keeping with the media and communication theme there are numerous instances of multimedia sound and video clips scattered throughout the site. Professor Chandler's selection of links also betrays a clear cultural interpretive bent and thus affords a solid introduction to this burgeoning movement and school within communication studies. Another fine general resource is maintained by the University of Iowa's Department of Communication Studies at **http://www.uiowa.edu/~commstud/links.html**.

MCS: The Media and Communication Studies Site
http://www.aber.ac.uk/~dgc/media.html

This rich site comes to us courtesy of Professor Daniel Chandler of the University of Wales, Aberystwyth. Although the site originates from the U.K., it draws liberally from U.S. links and

Mega Media-Links
http://www.rtvf.nwu.edu/links/

The creator of this site, Omnibus-eye media, is a spin-off from the Department of Radio, Television, and Film, Northwestern University. The Media-Links page is devoted to all aspects of broadcast media, film, radio, television, video and other new digital media. The site boasts over 3,500 links, so it is a good thing that there is an internal search engine that scans the entire site. It also has a formal arrangement formed around are dubbed *General Categories,* including *PRODUCTION: Resources and Info, COMPANIES and PRODUCTS, FESTIVALS and CONFERENCES, DIGITAL and NEW MEDIA, BROADCASTING: HISTORY, STUDIES and EDUCATION, DATABASES and INFORMATION, MOVIES, TV SHOWS and STARS, NEWS, REVIEWS and THEATERS,* etc. Each of the categories, in turn, is divided into subcategories such that the broad category *DATABASES and INFORMATION* has separate sections devoted to *FILM/MEDIA DATABASES, NATIONAL CINEMA and SPECIAL INTEREST SITES,* and *MEDIA LAW and REGULATION.* There is an alphabetized set of links under each of the subcategories and there is a brief but useful description attached to most of the links.

The range of links is truly astonishing. For instance, who would ever think that there is a database devoted to *Dermatology in the Cinema,* in which a practicing dermatologist explores the skin conditions of Hollywood stars. In short, Mega Media-Links offers something for virtually all tastes. One criticism of the site, however, is that many of the links need to be better maintained and updated.

The Media History Project: Promoting the Study of Media History from Petroglyphs to Pixels
http://www.mediahistory.com

This very fine multimedia site is maintained by Professor Kristina Ross, Department of Communication, University of Texas at El Paso. As the title suggests, the site is devoted to investigating the evolution of various forms of media. Professor Ross groups media into th-

irteen historical types, starting with *Oral Culture* and advancing to *Printing, Telegraph, Telephony, Journalism, Advertising, Radio, Movies, Recording Industry, Comics, Television Computing,* and *What's Fun* or alternative media. Each group is divided into a number of topical areas. For instance, *Radio* has individual categories for *Museums & Institutional Resources, General Broadcast History Resources, Stations, Networks & Companies, Programs & Pioneers,* and *International Radio.*

Many of the radio sites feature sound and, likewise, the television and movie links boast video clips. In addition, to the historical categories there are also separate entries for a glossary of key concepts and theorists, a huge time line from 45,000 bc to the present and links to professional organizations, journals, and syllabi related to media history. All in all, the project does an excellent job of showcasing the instructional potential of the web as a newcomer to the field of media studies.

Ed Lamoreux: Rhetorical Resources
http://bradley.bradley.edu/~ell

Professor Lamoreux, Department of Communication, Bradley University, constructed this site in conjunction with an online course he developed, *Theory and Literature of Rhetoric.*

The course and the site itself are divided into two main components: *Notes* and *Links*. The former is comprised of a series of more than forty lectures and lecture outlines of varying length and depth. The lectures or notes range from pre-Socratic rhetoric to contemporary thinkers. All told, they offer a detailed summary of the course, and it is interesting to note the energy and sheer work that Professor Lamoreux has devoted to bringing his course online.

The external links related to rhetoric are equally impressive. The links are not presented in any logical or alphabetical kind of order, but they do a thorough job of surveying substantive sites dedicated to rhetoric. Another impressive site devoted to rhetoric is W. Scott Thune's **Bibliography for Rhetoric and Professional Communication** at **http://www.public.iastate .edu/~wsthune/research/bib1.html**. Also see Professor Gideon Burton's fine glossary of rhetoric, **The Forest of Rhetoric** at **http:// humanities.byu.edu/rhetoric/forest.htm**.

Douglass: Archives of American Public Address
http://douglass.speech.nwu.edu

This site is sponsored by the Department of Communication Studies, Northwestern University. In effect, it serves as a database of speech and oratory and is named after Frederick Douglass owing to his mastery of public address. The site is indexed in a number of different ways. There is a search form at the top of the page that allows for keyword searching of the entire site. There are also separate categories that enable one to locate items *By Speaker*, *By Title*, *Chronologically*, and *By Controversy/Movement*. The database is not particularly large, and features only 150 or so speeches. What does distinguish Douglass is the quality of the speeches and their handsome layout.

Most of the speeches emanate from the nineteenth century, and the majority are the issue of political figures. On the other hand, there are also some very recent addresses from the likes of Bill and Hillary Clinton. In addition to the speech database there is a useful section on *Speech Guides & Notes*, which provides historical context for the speeches, and also a *Reference* section furnishing valuable links to other sites exploring American public address. A longer and more diffuse list of speeches is available at **ACA Rhetoric and Public Address Library** at **http://www.uark. edu/depts/comminfo/www/rhetoric.html**.

NewsPlace for News and Sources

     N.E.W.S. [News, entertainment, weather, sports]
     SOURCES [Government, activist, travel, corporate]
     TOOLS [Resource, reference, search, locator]

NewsPlace for News and Sources
http://www.niu.edu/newsplace

This site is primarily devoted to journalism and is the creation of Professor Avi Bass, Communications Department, Northern Illinois University. The site is organized around three topical headings: *N.E.W.S., SOURCES,* and *TOOLS. N.E.W.S.* boasts an enormous number and range of sites. There are links to hundreds of newspapers, newsmagazines, and online news resources throughout the world. The *SOURCES* button provides access to breaking stories and primary resources. The latter include such entities as the White House Briefing Room, the Vatican, activist groups and think tanks covering the entire spectrum of political and ideological engagement. There is also a substantial area devoted to institutional and corporate news releases and an extensive section addressed to censorship issues. *TOOLS* not only furnishes common reference sources like directories, dictionaries, and a variety of search engines but also includes links to the most significant professional organizations and associations dedicated to journalism.

In addition, there are three separate categories dubbed *Web Skills* (links to guides on building web sites), *Northern Notes* (instructional and class materials), and *White House 2000* (a rich collection of materials focused on the upcoming Presidential election). Another highly recommended journalism resource is Robert Nile's **Finding Data on the Internet: A Journalist's Guide** at **http://nilesonline. com/data**.

The Media Literacy Online Project
http://interact.oregon.edu/ mediaLit/Homepage

This innovative site, hosted by the College of Education, University of Oregon, is founded on the idea of encouraging critical thinking about media's social role and influence. More specifically, the aim of the site, as stated by its editors, is to help students develop an "understanding of the nature of the mass media, the techniques used by them, and the impact of these techniques."

The site is divided into a number of major categories, including *Teacher's Desk, Issues: Media Literacy, Media Industry, Reading Resources, Parents Corner*, etc. Each of these categories, in turn, has a number of subdivisions with relevant links. For instance, the broad category devoted to the media industry has separate divisions ranging from *Advertising and Marketing* to *Photographic and Digital Media*. Individual subdivisions then present a well annotated list of relevant links. The annotations do not run more than a couple of sentences but are consistently useful and informative. Some of these lists are quite extensive, especially on hot button issues, such as media violence and censorship.

There is also a host of original materials, such as articles focused on some aspect of media literacy, and an entire series of research bibliographies that size up the literature on specific topics. The one drawback to the site is that it does not seem to have been updated on a regular basis of late.

IMDb Internet Movie Database

http://www.imdb.com

This extraordinary site is sponsored by the online bookstore Amazon.com. The scope of the database is truly impressive and encompasses over 150,000 titles, and a continually expanding filmography of more than 2 million entries. The main page features news and current events germane to film, and also a daily updated list of new releases.

The heart of the project, however, consists of the search engine that navigates the site. The search engine is simple, but very efficient. The database can be searched either by film title, or by name. The latter includes not only actors and directors, but also genres such as western of film noir. The astonishing part is the amount of information attached to each film. For instance, and this is not an isolated case, a search of the title *The Man Who Shot Liberty Valence* retrieved not only the full cast and crew (John Wayne, James Stewart, Vera Miles, Lee Marvin, etc.), but also complete biographies and filmographies of each of the actors. In addition, there was also a *plot summary*, and links to *external reviews, awards and nominations, posters*, etc. The index alone to a major director like Jean Renoir runs a full six pages. In short, IMDB offers a wealth of detailed information. Other places one might look for film links are the American Film Institute's massive directory entitled **CineMedia** at **http://afi.cinemedia.org**.

Economics

There is an old joke that economists tell, the gist of which is that good economists are reincarnated as physicists and that the bad are reincarnated as sociologists. This tale is emblematic of how economist's have distanced themselves from the other social sciences by attempting to emulate the rigor of the natural sciences. Nonetheless, economics as a discipline clearly falls within the purview of the social sciences, and if there is one trait that makes it stand out from the others, it is its overarching dependence on mathematics.

As a predictive and policy oriented science economics has proven as vulnerable as every other social science, but in terms of its theoretical sophistication and complexity of argument, it remains unrivaled. It is for this reason that economics is often difficult for the initiate and assumes a fair amount of prior knowledge. Despite the difficulties in approaching current economic thinking, a number of economists have put together marvelous web sites. Some of the best sites for retrieving economic data, such as the University of San Diego and the Inter-University Consortium for Political and Social Research (ICPSR), were mentioned in the previous chapter on the Social Sciences. This particular chapter will offer a general guide to the field and then focus on particular sub-disciplines and schools of economic thought.

Resources for Economists on the Internet

http://rfe.org

Professor Bill Goffe, Department of Economics and International Business, University of Southern Mississippi, has assembled one of the finest general guides of any discipline on the web. Professor Goffe presented his first version of the guide in 1993 and has revised and updated it numerous times since.

The full index to the guide runs thirteen pages and lists hundreds of sites. The links are

organized around thirty plus broad subject headings, including *U.S. Macro and Regional Data*, *Working Papers*, *On-Line Journals*, *Economic Societies and Associations*, *Single Subject Economic Sites*, *Statistical and Computational Software*, etc. Each of the individual links has been carefully selected and annotated for its information content. If one had to choose a single site devoted to economics than this would surely be the one. A somewhat differently organized but also exceptional guide to economics is **NetEc** located at **http://netec.wustl.edu/NetEc.html**

History of Economics Internet References

http://cfec.vub.ac.be/cfec/hope.htm

This site is the work of Professor Bert Mosselmans, Centre for Financial Economics, Free University of Brussels, Belgium. One way of introducing economics and economic thinking is via study of the discipline's history, and in particular its formative thinkers.

Professor Mosselmans has assembled a broad canvas of the great movers and shakers in economics. The site is divided into nine separate subject areas, but the heart of it revolves around the major schools of economic thought: *Classical Political Economy*, *Marxism*, *Neoclassical Economics*, and *Keynesianism*. Under each of these categories are sites devoted to the individual thinkers attached to that particular school. It varies from figure to figure, but generally one finds a short biography or profile, an assessment of the contribution to economics as a discipline, and an excerpt or complete edition of one of the author's most salient works. For instance, under John Maynard Keynes one finds a complete edition of his early work, *The Economic Consequences of the Peace*, whereas for Marx, one finds a full-text version of *Capital, Vol. 1*. The site is easy to navigate, and affords an opportunity to browse a host of the major works that have contributed to the formation of economics as a distinctive discipline.

Economic Time Series Page

http://bos.business.uab.edu/data/ data.htm

Professor Ted Bos, School of Business, University of Alabama at Birmingham, developed this very useful page. Economists often employ large time series data in formulating and testing their arguments, and as we have seen there are huge compilations of these data sets at ICPSR and the University of San Diego. The problem with many of these data sets is that they can be cumbersome to download and cannot, in any case, be viewed and printed immediately from the web.

Professor Bos has assembled a number of data sets that not only can be retrieved on screen from a web browser, but furnish vertical and horizontal charts of the data. Currently, the time series available (Professor Bos intends to add more) are: *Monthly and Quarterly Federal Reserve Data, Business Cycle Indicators, Survey of Current Business*, and *Employment and Unemployment Data*. Within each one of these categories there are hundreds of statistical series. All in all, there are data and charts for over 75,000 series. This is a very neat and painless way of extracting economic data. Professor Bos has also included a substantial list of links to other sites that provide time series data. These sites include, for instance, *Bureau of Census, Bureau of Labor Statistics*, a number of individual *Federal Reserve Banks, Monthly Consumer Price Indexes, Monthly Exchange Rate Data*, etc.

http://ideas.uqam.ca/QMRBC

This page is maintained by Professor Christian Zimmermann, Department of Economics, University of Quebec, Montreal. This site is not perhaps for freshman, but it does take a broad and multi-sided view of what macroeconomic theory can tell us about the incidence of business cycles.

The homepage is organized around twenty-five broad topical categories. There is an interesting mix of original material and external links. Professor Zimmermann has posted a number of his own research papers and projects and has also included a substantial bibliography of the field. The bibliography alone attests to the value of the site and weighs in with over 634 citations. In addition, there are categories linked to *Books, Readings, Data, Software, Research Centers, Working Papers,* etc. For the initiate there is a thoughtful definition and discussion, courtesy of UCLA Professor Gary Hansen, of real business cycles under the heading of *Meaning*. Although Professor Zimmerman's pitch is primarily aimed at practitioners in the field, there is still a good deal of worthwhile material for the student and curious lurker.

http://www.oswego.edu/~kane/ econometrics

This site was developed by Professor John Kane, Department of Economics, State University of New York-Oswego. Professor Kane is currently working on a text, *Econometrics: An Applied Approach* (forthcoming, 1999), and has placed materials on the web as an adjunct to the text. However, the site stands very well on its own.

As the name implies, econometrics involves the application of mathematical and statistical modeling techniques to economic activity and behavior. Even more so than other areas of economics, econometrics requires substantial background knowledge. Professor Kane's page fortunately is oriented equally to the student and practitioner. The site is well organized around fifteen broad subject categories, including *Data Sources, Economic Institutes and Research Organizations, Federal and State Government Sites, International Agencies*, etc. Of particular interest is his critical and comprehensive set of links to *Econometric Software* specifically designed to be employed in the development of models.

Al Roth's game theory
and experimental economics page

http://www.economics.harvard.edu/ ~aroth/alroth.html

Professor Roth occupies the prestigious chair of George Gund Professor of Economics and Business Administration, Department of Economics, Harvard University. In short, he is a major figure in the field of game theory and experimental economics. Essentially, Professor Roth's work involves mathematical modeling of interdependent decision making, in which the choices made by one party impacts all the other parties involved in the game. There are abundant examples where game theory can be applied, such as bargaining between labor unions and management, different firms competing in the same market, and so forth.

Game theory is by no means restricted to economics but is perhaps pursued more aggressively in this field than others. In any case, Professor Roth presents us with a wealth of both introductory and specialist original material and an abundance of his own writings. The site is divided into thirteen broad categories, including background on the history and methodology of game theory, and there are also articles, abstracts, working papers, bibliographies, experiments conducted on both the web and the classroom, and links to other game theory servers. Professor Roth vividly conveys his passion for game theory, and makes a strong argument in favor of of alotting a higher profile to game theory for the social sciences in general.

Economic Growth Resources

http://www.nuff.ox.ac.uk/ Economics/Growth

This site was developed by Professor Jonathan Temple, Junior Research Fellow in Economics, Hertford College, Oxford. Professor Temple's page is primarily oriented toward the field of developmental economics, or the study of the economies of developing nations and what factors encourage or impede growth in those economies.

Developmental economics is a huge and vital field of activity for economists and policy makers of all stripes. Professor Temple has established a very fine set of eleven topical areas circumscribing the field. The categories include heading such as, *Data sets, Growth/ development links, Latest research, Literature surveys, World Bank Economic Growth Project*, etc. Of particular note are the marvelous searchable databases *Penn World Tables* and *Social Indicators of Development*. Each of these statistical databases surveys every economy in the world, and allows one to plug in discrete factors, such as gross national product, or mortality, and see how individual nations stack up. Both databases can be found under *Data sets*.

Professor Temple has also compiled some very fine bibliographies to orient the novice or seasoned researcher in the field of developmental economics. The bibliographies are located under the headings *Key references, Latest research*, and *Literature surveys*. In addition, to Professor Temple's page one might also consult Professor Giorgio Secondi's web site **Development Economics and Economic Development** at **http://www-personal.umich. edu/~giosecco/dev.html**

http://www.igc.org/igc/labornet

Unfortunately, there are not any sites devoted exclusively to two of the most significant economic subdisciplines, labor and welfare economics. This site, sponsored by the activist agency, Institute for Global Communications, is dedicated to unions, labor and worker's welfare as opposed to labor or welfare economics proper.

The site furnishes current events, news reporting, and editorials for labor activists and the like. There is also a button focused squarely on economics and economic issues of interest to labor. As one might imagine, the tone is partisan, and decidedly leftish, which is not a bad thing considering the conservative slant of many academic economics departments. In any case, the editors have compiled dozens of sites with arch-progressive views on economic issues. There are links to think tanks, institutes, proposed legislation, full-text journal articles etc. The two most common themes running throughout the links are an anticorporate and pro-ecological stance, yet at the same time there is a wide variety of opinion expressed. The chief virtue of the site is that it opens a window to the workings of radical economics and the dissenting academy.

Education

Teachers were among the first professional groups to pursue and explore the web as a vehicle for delivering educational materials and instruction. As a consequence, there has been an explosion of web sites developed by professional educators. Indeed, every site in this volume could be brought under the rubric educational.

The focus of this chapter is on education as an applied social science. Particular emphasis is placed on educational research and teacher training and classroom resources. In addition, some of the more significant subfields within the discipline, like school psychology and special education, will be addressed. Despite this narrow definition of education there is still a tremendous number and diversity of sites. New fields, like distance education, have paralleled the growth of the web, and one can only expect that the web will play an increasingly important role as both a teaching tool and a forum for educators to test new ideas and forge closer bonds.

AskERIC: Education Information with the Personal Touch
http://ericir.syr.edu

This marvelous site is hosted by Syracuse University and is federally funded under the auspices of the Department of Education. One could not ask more of a general site surveying web resources on education. ERIC is the acronym for Education Resources Information Center. It was originally assembled in 1967 as a comprehensive paper index to education research, and continues to fulfill a very valuable service in that area.

As this site attests, ERIC has expanded much beyond its original indexing function. There are three essential components of Ask-ERIC: *Question & Answer Service*, *Virtual Library*, and the *ERIC Database* itself. The *Question & Answer Service* is an online reference desk aimed at professional educators who have questions regarding educational research or the practice of education. The only other limitation is that one must have an E-mail account. There is a detailed form for queries, and the patron is assured an E-mail response from an ERIC information specialist within 48 hours. If one wants to sleuth independently one can turn to the other two components of Ask-ERIC. The *Virtual Library* has several categories of information resources including, a *Toolbox, InfoGuides, Lesson Plans, Television Series Companion Materials,* etc. Each of these categories feature a different type of resource, but when taken together they offer a broad perspective on the whole array of educational materials available over the web.

The *ERIC Database* is an unparalleled tool for exploring educational research and practice. Although the database does not date back to the beginnings in 1967, it does include approximately a quarter million citations from the present back to 1989. There are two halves of the database encompassing both an index to periodical literature and so-called ERIC documents including, such material as speeches at conferences, association reports, and federal, state, and local educational studies. The Syracuse site features a well-articulated and serviceable search form for the database, and it is a tremendous benefit to have ERIC so readily available. If interested in further exploring general web guides to educational resources see also **The Cisco Educational Archive and Resources Catalog** at **http://sunsite.unc.edu/cisco**, or the outstanding Australian site, **Education Internet Guide: Sources for Theory, Practice, Teaching and Research** at **http://www.library.usyd.edu.au/Guides/Education/index.html**.

Blue Web'n: A Library of Blue Ribbon Learning sites

http://www.kn.pacbell.com/wired/bluewebn

This site is an outgrowth of a project undertaken by communications giant Pacific Bell in conjunction with San Diego State University's Department of Educational Technology. The overarching goal here is to select the best web resources employing the Internet for instructional purposes.

Virtually all disciplines and all levels of instruction are included, but the majority of links are to K-12 instruction. There are a number of ways in which one can specify the level and type of teaching material one seeks, but the easiest and most direct method is to employ what the creators of the site dub their *Applications Table*. The table consists of a grid that lists individual disciplines vertically and separate types of applications (lesson plans, activities, projects, tools, etc.) horizontally. In addition, the grid indicates how many items are available in a particular category. For instance, if one clicks on *Health & Physical Education* and *Resources,* one will find twenty-three items to choose from. Each resource is provided with a solid description, and rated from one to five stars (the majority of links are five star sites). If one wants to explore how to incorporate the Internet into one's own teaching and curriculum then Blue Web'n points out a host of wonderful opportunities. Another technology driven new field is so-called Distance Education. An excellent guide for for the field is **DLRN: Distance Learning Resource Net-**work at **http://www.wested.org/tie/dlrn**.

NATIONAL CENTER FOR EDUCATION STATISTICS

NCES Products: Electronic Catalog and On-line Library

http://nces.ed.gov/

Education would hardly qualify as a social science if it did not generate mounds of statistics, and the best place to locate and retrieve current educational statistics is the Department of Education's National Center for Education Statistics. Here are located hundreds of publications statistically profiling the U.S. educational system from every imaginable vantage point.

The initial page features a number of categories including, *Electronic Catalog*, *Survey and Program Areas*, *Data Acess Tools*, *Fast Facts*, etc. Each of these categories lists publications generally according to release date. Looking at individual titles typically offers directions on of how to download the text or how to purchase a hard copy. Moreover, most titles have tables, charts, bars, and graphs illustrating the contents of that particular title.

The most significant category of NCES publications is *The Digest, The Condition, and other compendia*. Both *The Digest of Educational Statistics* and *The Condition of Education* are annual reports representing baseline information on the status of U.S. education. The former represents a broad outline of educational statistics ranging from kindergarten to graduate school, whereas the latter is a federally mandated report to Congress that attempts to achieve a consensus view on the progress of U.S. education. The NCES is a rich empirical resource for any one thinking of conducting educational research.

Developing Educational Standards

http://putwest.boces.org/standards.html

Educational standards are a hot-button issue in the field, and this fine site was assembled by Charles West, in conjunction with Putnam Valley Schools, Putnam Valley, New York. In the simplest sense, standards aim at furnishing an objective measure of student achievement, yet as this page attests, there is a great deal of discussion and debate on how to establish and verify the objectivity of such measures.

The site is divided into three essential components: *Government and general resources, Standards and frameworks documents.* The latter have separate indexes for both subject and state. Each link within the categories is provided with an impressive gloss explaining precisely the type and significance of information being offered. There is also a substantial amount of full-text and original material available. Under the first category, one finds not only information on state and federal projects, but there is also a host of initiatives undertaken by indepependant laboratories, clearinghouses, and professional organizations. The second category offers a list of recommended standards according to individual disciplines, ranging from *Art and Music* to *Technology.* The third category offers a directory organized around individual states and details standards implemented from Alabama to Wyoming. Another site that approaches standards and assessment from a somewhat different angle is **Assessment and Evaluation on the Internet** at **http://ericae.net/intbod.stm**.

School Psychology Resources
online

http://www.bcpl.lib.md.us/ ~sandyste/school_psych.html

This site is the creation of Dr. Sandra Steingart of the Office of Psychological Services, Baltimore County Public Schools, Towson, Maryland. School psychology as an independent discipline involves the psychological evaluation and assessment of students intellectual, emotional/behavioral, and social development.

Dr. Steingart's site provides a fine over-overview of the many activities in which school psychologists are engaged. The home-page is divided into two broad categories:

Specific Conditions, Disorders, Handicaps, and *Other Information.* The first category has separate headings for *Anxiety Disorders, Medical Conditions, Substance Abuse, Mental Retardation, Suicide, Autism, Learning Disabilities,* etc., whereas the second category addresses more general societal issues such as *Adolescence, Violence, Parenting and Family, Mental Health,* and the like. Under each heading, there is a short list of one to ten carefully selected sites. The aim is not to be as comprehensive as possible, but rather to furnish an efficient means of channeling queries to the most direct source on the issue. For a broader view of the entire field of educational psychology see **Educational Psychology Topics** at **http://www. mhhe.com/socsscience/education/edpsych/ edpsytop.html**.

Special Education Resources on the Internet

SERI: Special Education Resources on the Internet
http://www.hood.edu/seri/serihome. htm

This site, hosted by the Special Education Department, Hood College, Maryland, covers some of the same ground as the one on school psychology. However, this site focuses much more squarely on disability issues. Links are grouped under twenty-two separate categories starting with *General Disabilities Information,* and concluding with *Transition Resources.*

Most of the categories focus on specific disabilities, such as mental retardation, attention deficit disorder, speech, hearing and vision impairment, etc. Individual sites within a category are often furnished with a brief description and afford a broad array of information, ranging from original articles to directories to online databases. Although the primary focus is on disabilities, one area that also falls within the realm of special education is gifted education. There are a limited number of links to gifted education, but if this is a particular area of interest see, the **National Center for Gifted Education & Talent Development** at **http://www.gifted.uconn.edu/**.

Explorations in Learning & Instruction:
The Theory Into Practice Database

Learning & Instruction:
The TIP Database

http://www.gwu.edu/~tip

This interesting and wholly original site was created by Professor Greg Kearsley of George Washington University's School of Education and Human Development. The principal aim of the site is to explore the many positions and arguments advanced in the field of learning theory.

Learning theory addresses the question of how we learn and what agents are most significant in spurring and encouraging learning. Professor Kearsley has divided his site into three essential components: *Theories, Learning Domains*, and *Learning Concepts*. Under the first category are listed fifty distinct learning theories. Clicking on *Constructivist Theory*, for instance, retrieves a brief essay offering an overview of the theory and a bibliography for further reading. It is interesting to note the extremely broad array of competing theories. The second category, *Learning Domains*, focuses on different functional areas of learning, such as decision making, language, problem solving, reading, etc. Again, each functional area is furnished with a concise essay and references. The third area, *Learning Concepts*, deals with notions such as attention, creativity, intelligence, motivation and the like. Here, one also finds solid overviews with references. Taken as a whole, the TIP Database offers a substantial introduction and panoramic view of the field of learning theory.

Geography

The discipline of geography aims at describing and analyzing natural and human variation across the globe. Within this very broad framework, spatial organization takes a leading role in geographic explanation. There are three central geographic subdisciplines: physical geography, human geography, and regional geography. Each of these subdisciplines has its own distinct history and methods. For instance, physical geography has very close ties to geology and the physical sciences. In this chapter, we will veer away from the more purely geologic and earth science aspects of the field. On the other hand, human geography is of ancient lineage and has closes ties to fields like history, ethnography, and travel.

Geography, like so many other social science disciplines, has also greatly benefitted from technological innovations, allowing for the emergence of such fields as computerized geographic information systems and remote sensing imagery collected from satellites. In short, geography is an exciting and catholic discipline that continues to expand the tools employed and subject matter coverage.

Geography, Geology & Meteorology

CTI (Computers in Teaching Initiative): Centre for Geography, Geology & Meteorology

http://www.geog.le.ac.uk/cti/index.html

This model site is hosted by the Department of Geography at the University of Leicester, U.K. Although geology and meteorology are included in the title, the primary focus is on geography proper. In order to explore the CTI links, click on the bar for *Information Gateway* at the bottom of the homepage. This retrieves a index of the various subdisciplines within geography including *Human Geography, Physical Geography, Cartography, Geographic Information Systems, Place Information, Planning and Transportation*, and so forth.

Clicking on one of the subdisciplines retrieves an index of the fields within the subdiscipline. For instance, clicking on *Human Geography* calls up eleven fields ranging, from *Agriculture,* to *Economic Geography,* to *Urban Geography.* Clicking on the field then retrieves a list of sites divided between European and non-European resources. Generally, each field lists ten to fifteen resources. CTI does not aim at comprehensiveness in terms of the numbers of sites listed. However, the series of hierarchical indexes furnishes a accurate outline of the range of activities involved in geographic research. In this regard, CTI provides an ideal starting point for exploring geography on the web. Another general site that has a huge load of links, but is somewhat cluttered is **Geography at the Mining Company** at **http://geography.miningco.com**.

Cartographic Resources on the WWW

http://leardo.lib.uwm.edu/other.html

Cartography is one of the most ancient and vital fields of geography, and this impressive site is an offshoot of the American Geographical Society Collection, housed at the University of Wisconsin-Milwaukee Library.

The homepage is divided into seven categories representing different types and sources for maps and cartographic information. The first category is *Comprehensive URLographies in Cartography*, followed by *General Reference Mappers, U.S. Government Map Resources, Map Libraries, Regional Maps* (other than U.S.), *Commercial Map Resources*, and *Other Resources*. Each category lists six to ten sites. For example, the general reference category includes map directories, road and travel maps, weather maps and U.S. census maps. The other categories furnish even more specialized information, ranging from historical maps, to environmental and geologic maps, to satellite images. The only problem with the site is that a number of links have been allowed to lapse indicating a need for more timely maintenance. For a marvelous collection of historical maps, see the University of Texas' **Perry-Castañeda Library Map Collection** at **http://www.lib. utexas.edu/Libs/PCL/Map_collection/ historical/history_main.html**.

Color Landform Atlas of the United States

http://fermi.jhuapl.edu/states/states. html

This site was created by Senior Mathematician Ray Sterner of the Space Oceanography Group, Johns Hopkins University. Mr. Sterner offers a unique online atlas of each of the states. Clicking on a state allows one to choose a *Shaded relief map*, *County map*, *Satellite image*, downloadable *Postscript map*, or in many cases an historic *1895 map*.

With the exception of the latter, these are all landform maps, so they do not indicate cities, highways, etc. On the other hand, the landform images provide a beautiful survey of the topography and vegetation patterns of each of the states. Mr. Sterner also furnishes a good deal of technical information on the composition and coding involved in reproducing the maps. In addition, there are eighteen external links furnishing detailed information about the state. Here one finds a directory to state and national parks, regional data from the Environmental Protection Agency and the U.S. Geological Survey, and also information about cities, weather and current news about the state. The site is easy to navigate and affords hours of captivating browsing.

Great GIS Net Sites!

http://www.gisportal.com/

GIS is the acronym for Geographic Information Systems, which is one of geography's hottest fields. This comprehensive site with over 700 links is supported by Harvard Design and Mapping Company, Cambridge, Massachusetts. GIS are employed in complex planning and management problems that link spatial issues with other data sets. For example, GIS applications are involved in questions ranging from long range environmental planning to where to situate a shopping mall in a particular community.

Typically, a GIS requires a computer and sophisticated software in which various types or combinations of data are overlaid on a map. This site divides GIS resources into twenty-two categories, including *Site of the Month*, *GIS News*, *Classic GIS Sites*, *Online GIS*, *GIS WWW Resources*, *GIS Data and Software Library*, *GIS Services*, etc. Each category presents an alphabetized list of pertinent links. There is rarely a description of the contents of sites and there is a general assumption that those visiting the site are familiar with GIS terms and applications. However, for the novice there is an excellent FAQ defining GIS under the category *Classic GIS Sites*. GIS is a rapidly expanding field, and this site helps explain why.

STARTING THE HUNT

Guide To On-line And Mostly Free U.S. Geospatial and Attribute Data

http://www.cast.uark.edu/local/ hunt/index.html

Despite the prolix title, this is an extremely valuable and ingenious site. It was designed by Stephan Pollard of the Center for Advanced Spatial Technologies (CAST), University of Arkansas. There are links to hundreds of maps and other geographic data. However, what is truly exceptional about Mr. Pollard's work is the elaborate classification scheme he has imposed on the links.

Under the category *Subject-Oriented List*, there is an alphabetized catalog of topics, including *Agriculture, Census, Ecology, Hazardous Substance, Land Use and Land Cover, Political and Administrative, Transportation*, and several others. Located under each of these topics, in turn, is a list of resources. Many of the items are located at various federal agencies, yet it would demand an immense amount of time to collect each of these items individually. Mr. Pollard has performed a signal service by bringing sense and order to what is clearly widely dispersed information.

U.S. Gazetteer

http://www.census.gov/ cgi-bin/gazetteer

GEOnet Names Server

http://164.214.2.59/gns/html/index. html

Both of these sites identify geographic place names. The first, sponsored by the Census Bureau, is aimed at U.S. place names, whereas the second, sponsored by the National Imagery and Mapping Agency, focuses on international place names.

The U.S. Gazetteer has a query form on the homepage in which one can type a name, state, zip code, or all three. The search retrieves counties, townships or cities, and indicates population, latitude and longitude, and zip codes. In addition, the search affords the option of viewing TIGER maps of the area and 1990 census data. TIGER is the acronym for Topologically Integrated Geographic Encoding and Referencing System, and furnishes highly detailed and customizable map images. For instance, one can zoom in and zoom out, changing the scale of the map, and one can add features like highways, streets, railroads, shorelines, parks, and other geographically nottable features of the community. Clicking a separate button retrieves a broad selection of census data, which is also customizable. In short, this is one powerful gazetteer that has relevance far beyond merely geographic information.

On the other hand, the GEOnet Names Server furnishes place names for all nations other than the U.S. The database has over 3.3 million entries, and although it does not possess mapping or census figures, it does furnish a broad array of geographic information. There are a number of ways to query the database.

One can simply type in the name of a city or community, or there is a form from which one can select a designated nation and another set of nine forms devoted to feature designations, such as road/railroad features, hypsographic features, vegetation features, etc. There is also a form that allows one to locate communities within specific latitudinal and longitudinal coordinates. For instance, one can locate the capital of Lithuania, by selecting the form for countries, and then selecting *Capital of a Political Entity* from the form for *Populated Place Features*. Not only does one find that Vilnius is the proper name for Vilna but that there are six other variations for the name of the capital of Lithuania. One can also do things like locate areas designated as beaches in Mexico or coconut groves in Fiji. The options are virtually limitless.

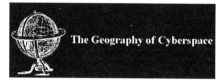

http://www.geog.ucl.ac.uk/casa/ martin/geography_of_cyberspace. html

This fascinating site designed by Research Fellow Martin Dodge of the Centre for Advanced Spatial Analysis, University College London, is devoted to mapping the Internet and understanding it as a geographic entity.

The site is divided into thirteen topical categories, at the top of which is *An Atlas of Cyberspace* compiled by Mr. Dodge. Here are located all kinds of graphic and spatial images of the web and the Internet. Many of the maps are stunning in the way they visually display the complexity of Internet networking. Other categories, include *Mapping the Internet, Visualizing WWW Space, Geography of the Information Society, Internet Traffic, Size and Demographic Statistics*, etc. Each link is furnished with a short description of its contents, and there is a wide variety of information available within each of the categories. In addition to maps there are many conference papers, journal articles, and links to tools and software applications for mapping the Internet. The exponential growth of the Internet has assured that mapping its multiform network configurations and researching its geography will play an increasingly significant role within the discipline.

History

No discipline has a broader sweep than history. As the systematic study of the past, there is literally nothing that does not fall within history's purview. The writing of history is an ancient pursuit, but as an academic discipline it emerged parallel with that of the social sciences in the nineteenth century. At the same time history has maintained close ties with the humanities, and frequently historians see themselves as having a foot in both camps.

Traditional academic history focused on politics, diplomacy, and great events, yet in the twentieth century there has been an explosion of subfields and divisions within the discipline that gives no sign of abating. For instance, vital and flourishing subfields like gender history or environmental history were hardly mentioned fifty or even twenty-five years ago. Moreover, in recent decades there has been a growing awareness of the significance of non-Western or non-European history.

There are many historians in a broad variety of fields working diligently to make available the riches of the past via the web, either through the transcription of primary materials or through historical analysis proper. However, owing to the huge expanse of historical enquiry it is difficult to offer a coherent and well-rounded image of the discipline. This chapter will focus on a few outstanding sites and attempt to convey an idea of the breadth and density of contemporary historical enquiry.

H-Net: Humanities and Social Sciences Online
http://h-net.msu.edu/

This site is supported by both Michigan State University and the National Endowment for the Humanities. The title is somewhat misleading, in that it seems to indicate that the coverage is much broader than just history. Although H-Net does touch upon other disciplines, the central and primary focus is on history.

Originally, H-Net arose out of a consortium of scholarly E-mail lists. Today that list includes nearly one hundred separate groups, and encompasses an enormous variety of regional, topical, and methodological orientations. For instance, there are groups that are devoted to African, Asian, and Latin American history, and topics range from business to women's history, and the methodological approaches extend from explorations in popular culture to traditional diplomatic history. Moreover, H-Net has expanded far beyond discussion groups. Under the heading *H-Net Reviews*, there is an entire section dedicated to reviewing new books in the field. The reviews are substantial and often written by leading authorities in the field. On occasion authors respond to reviews, and a scholarly dialogue ensues. The reviews date back to 1995 and count in the hundreds. There are several ways to locate reviews. One can search by author, title, date, or keyword, and one can also limit reviews to a specific discussion group or area of interest.

Under a separate heading for *Networks,* there is an index to the eighty odd discussion groups. Clicking on a discussion group for example, H-France retrieves a menu that allows one to search the group's discussion archive, browse the above mentioned book reviews, or more important explore a set of links to remote resources. The links are not exclusively history oriented but offer items of interest to anyone thinking of traveling or conducting research in France. Each of the resources listed for the individual groups is organized a bit differently, yet most of them furnish a set of links to remote resources.

One final way to search H-NET is to click on *H-Net Hypertext Links Database* under the category *Interact with H-Net.* Located here is an eclectic list of resources, ranging from primary sources like the *Civil War Diaries of Galutia York* to research centers such as the *Edwin O. Reischauer Institute of Japanese Studies.* There is also a very detailed query form that can be searched either by region, sub-discipline or affiliated organization. Although the *Hypertext Links* contain a wealth of interesting sites, I still prefer searching the remote sources attached to each discussion group under *Networks*. To my mind the latter retrieves a more relevant list of items tailored to one's specific interests. In any case, H-Net is a marvelous general site for historical resources. It may take a bit of digging to figure out the best way to navigate H-Net, but the effort will pay off handsome dividends. Another recommended general site for history is the mammoth **World Wide Virtual Library: History** maintained at**http://history.cc.ukans.edu/history/**.

EuroDocs:
Primary Historical Documents
From Western Europe --

http://www.lib.byu.edu/~rdh/ eurodocs

This site is maintained by Richard Hacken of the Harold B. Lee Library, Brigham Young University. A frequent demand of undergraduate students is to incorporate primary materials into their research papers. Mr. Hacken's site offers a marvelous means for searching and locating full-text online primary documents focused on European history.

EuroDocs is organized around twenty-five headings. All of the headings except two, *Medieval & Renaissance Europe* and *Europe as a Supernational Region,* represent an individual European nation. Clicking on a nation retrieves a list of documents arranged in chrononological order. Documents have been transcribed, reproduced in facsimile, or trans slated. For instance, Ireland includes Edmund Spenser's *A View of the Present State of Ireland* (1596), along with a *History of the Irish Potato Famine*, and a transcribed version of the 1990 *Irish Constitution*. Obviously, certain nations like France, Germany and the United Kingdom have more materials than nations like Portugal. However, Mr. Hacken has been indefatigable in chasing down documents from every corner of Western Europe.

Of particular interest is the category of *Europe as a Supernational Region*. Here are located primary materials relating to wars and diplomacy and fundamental texts relating to the Maastricht Treaty. There are many other historical sites on the web that feature primary documents, yet very few have the depth and breadth of this collection. It should serve as a model for regions and topical areas other than Europe.

http://lcweb2.loc.gov/amhome.html

This magnificent site is the product of a cooperative venture spearheaded by the Library of Congress. Like the previous site it is oriented toward primary materials, yet it is not restricted to text but has full multimedia capabilities, including photos and prints, video and sound.

The homepage at first glance appears complicated, and it takes a while to gain one's bearings. At the top of the page there are three prominent categories: *Search*, *Browse*, and *Learn*. Clicking on *Learn* retrieves a number of guides and pathfinders on how the site is structured and suggestions on terms to employ in searching the database. The *Browse* button allows a variety of options, the most important of which is *Titles*. Clicking on *Titles* retrieves a complete list of the collections. At present, there are more than forty separate thematic collections, with the promise of a continuous flow of new additions.

To view a collection, for instance, the first one listed, *African American Perspectives: Pamphlets from the Daniel A.P. Murray Collection, 1818-1907*, click on the title and then retrieve individual items either through a keyword search, or through perusing an accompanying subject index. If one is new to the site, the *Browse* category is probably the best way to explore American Memory. Keep in mind that some of these collections are huge and contain tens of thousands of items. The more adventurous might try the *Search* category, which functions simply as a keyword search of the entire database. Avoid using search terms that are too general. For example, the search term *Oklahoma* alone retrieves more than 300 items. It is easy to get lost in American Memory, but then one might consider that one of its greatest strengths. It is a fascinating and rich site. Another fine collection of primary materials on the United States, although limited to the period 1850-1877, can be found at **The Making of America** at **http:// www.umdl.umich.edu/moa**.

Non-Western History

http://www.execpc.com/~dboals/ hist.html

This site was created by Dennis Boals, and is only a portion of a much larger site dedicated to K-12 social studies teachers. The K-12 tag might make it appear that the site falls outside the purview of this work, yet there is a good deal of material here of interest to those who have advanced far beyond secondary school. Moreover, at this time there is not anything comparable on the web focused directly on non-Western history.

Increasingly, historians are recognizing the need to view their discipline from a global perspective. However, the vast bulk of historical research has been dedicated to Western civilization, and this is well reflected in the historical sites posted on the web. This site helps to redress the balance. Mr. Boals has organized the site in a simple and straightforward manner. It is divided into seven categories: *Asia/Pacific, Central/South America, China/Japan, Africa, Middle East, India*, and *General/Cross-Cultural*. Under each category are listed a number of links, which appear to be listed in the order in which they were added to the list. In any case, browsing is not that onerous, in that the maximum number of links to any category is approximately 130. Again, although there are significant web sites that are devoted to each of these regions or areas (and the most prominent of these are included here), there are few sites that draw together as broad a range of materials as has Mr. Boals. Another valuable and even more extensive web site that covers both Western and non-Western history is the **Gateway to World History** at **http:// library.ccsu.ctstateu.edu/~history/world_ history/**.

ANCIENT WORLD WEB

http://www.julen.net/aw/

This comprehensive site was created by Julia Hayden. Unlike many other sites that focus on the ancients, this one does not restrict itself to just Aegean and Middle Eastern civilizations but rather encompasses the entire globe.

The Ancient World Web is effectively organized, and the bulk of the information is located under three central categories. Under *Geographical Organization*, there is a well articulated index of geographic regions. For instance, *Middle and Near East* includes separate categories for *Akkadia, Assyria, Israel, Jerusalem, Jordan, Levant, Persia, Sumer*, and *Syria*. Clicking on *Subject Organization* retrieves a list of broad topical areas, starting with *Ancient Documents* and concluding with *Towns, Cities and Other Places*. There is also a *Meta-Index* that alphabetically lists all the links within the Ancient World Web. To give an idea of the extent of the site, the complete index is over twenty pages long. As with the other categories each of the individual links is furnished with a brief annotation. For a look at a more abbreviated list of outstanding sites on the Ancient and Medieval world see **Argos** at **http://argos.evansvill.edu**.

The Labyrinth:

Resources for Medieval Studies

http://www.georgetown.edu/ labyrinth/

This appealing site is sponsored by Georgetown University and is co-directed by Martin

Irvine and Deborah Everhart. It has established a high standard for medieval web resources. The Labyrinth is divided into eight broad categories. *The Labyrinth Library* contains both medieval primary documents and contemporary secondary sources. For instance, clicking on *Old English* retrieves a set of documents among which one finds a copy of the British Library's *Beowulf* manuscript. The category of *Subjects* is subdivided into *National Cultures*, *International Culture*, and *Special Topics*. Here are located links to materials relating to Iberia, philosophy and theology, and chivalry.

Two other principal categories are *Pedagogical Resources*, and *Medieval Studies, Text, Image, and Archival Databases*. For the former there are instructions for teaching Latin and the like, and the latter offers a broad array of links to primary materials and research on medieval literature. The Labyrinth also has its own internal search engine. Another highly recommended site for medieval studies is the **ORB: The Online Reference Book for Medieval Studies** at **http://orb.rhodes.edu**.

Labour and Business History

http://www.iisg.nl/~w3vl/

Social history has unquestionably been the most dynamic subdiscipline within the field in the last twenty years. Unfortunately, there has yet to be created a site that attempts to serve as a clearinghouse for the massive variety of materials and research that fall under the rubric of social history. This site, however, maintained at Amsterdam by the International Institute for Social History and the Netherlands Economic History Archive, covers an area fundamental to the rise of contemporary social history.

In broad terms, social history arose as a reaction against the traditional historical emphasis on high politics and great events. Labor history bucked this tradition, and gradually there emerged a new concept of "history from below." The new paradigm focused on the working world of common people and their everyday lives and struggles. In any case, labor historians were instrumental in giving direction to social history.

Although this particular site is focused primarily on labor and business, it reaches out in many other directions. On the homepage there is a button for *Resources*, under which are listed approximately 300 sites. The links are grouped under eight headings, including *Labour History, Business and Economic History, Other History and Social Science Sites, Special Topics, Exhibitions*. There is good stuff on all aspects of labor, business, and economic history, but the remainder of the site is kind of a melange of general historical information and some interesting curiosities, like the *Utah Anarchism and Revolution Page*. This site does a good job of opening the door to social history, but there is still a need for a page that attempts to address social history in a broader and more comprehensive manner.

http://www.nwhp.org

A parallel and related development to the rise of social history was the advent of women's history, which today is surely one of the most active and innovative subfields within the discipline.

The interest in women's history has spawned a number of nonprofit educational organizations like the National Women's History Project. Their homepage explains what the organization is about and the broad field of activities in which they are involved. Of particular interest is the section *Important History Links*. The section is divided into thirteen separate categories, including *General/Overview, Women's Rights, Politics, African-American Women, Math and Science, War and Peace, State-Specific Resources, Sites for In-Depth Research*. Each individual link is furnished with a brief description, and there are all kinds of materials here, such as primary documents, encyclopedias, calendars, bibliographies, essays, and multimedia exhibits. It is clear that the National Women's History Project has been very choosy in selecting sites that offer a well-rounded image of current research in women's history.

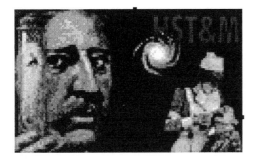

History of Science, Technology and Medicine

http://www.asap.unimelb.edu.au/ hstm/hstm_ove.htm

Traditionally, the history of science was the preserve of scientists themselves. This has radically changed in the last few decades as historians of all stripes have come to appreciate the central role of the development of the sciences in shaping the modern world.

This impressive site is maintained by Tim Sherratt for the Australian Science Archives Project (ASAP). The site is divided into ten broad categories, including *Organisations and Conferences*; *Specialised Collections and Documents*; *Biographical Dictionary*; *Historical Directory of Scientific Institutions and Organisations*; *Museums Exhibitions and Images*; *Other lists; Collections and Bibliographies*.

The heart of the enterprise is located under the category of *Specialised Collections and Documents*. Here each of the sciences and corollary fields are listed alphabetically with corresponding links. For instance, there are separate entries for *Astronomy and Space, Biology, Chemistry, Early Science and Alchemy, Geology and Mining, Medicine and Health, Scientific Instruments, Technology, Women Scientists*, and several others. Each of the subject areas has a select set of links, some of which are surprising and unique such as the very fine *British Lawnmower Museum* listed under the category of *Technology*.

In addition, do not overlook the extensive and scholarly *Biographical Dictionary* and the marvelous entries listed under *Museums, Exhibitions and Images*. Another fine site, although on a smaller scale, is the **History of Science** at **http://weber.u.washington.edu/ mudrock/HISTORY/science.html**.

Political Science and Government

The academic discipline of political science aims at analyzing and explaining the nature and dynamic of political activity and power. Like the other social sciences it draws from a variety of disciplines such as economics, history psychology and sociology, and represents a wide array of divergent theoretical and methodological outlooks.

Political science in its most traditional guise is strongly philosophical and addresses questions like, "What constitutes the good society?" At the other end of the spectrum are public administration and public policy analysts asking nuts and bolts questions about the costs benefits of a particular piece of legislation or regulation. Another area of major interest is the field of international relations and diplomacy, yet even here there are stark contrasts in the way different practitioners approach the field. On the one hand, there are moralists who attempt to establish just and ethical procedures for arbitrating international questions, whereas there is also a realist school that argues that states naturally follow their own self interest and that analysis should focus on balance-of-power relations. In any case, political science is a vibrant discipline whose many facets are a testament to its continued growth and ability to attract talented practitioners.

This chapter will be someone different than previous ones in that the focus will be not only on political science but also on government resources. In particular, emphasis will be laid on the incomparable riches of U.S. government web resources. The U.S. government has been a pioneer in posting vital public information on the web, and it would be a severe oversight not to give it due credit. Many states and local authorities following the federal government's lead have also been energetic in posting information. Indeed, the number of government sites is now overwhelming. What will be attempted here is to offer a rough outline on the essential resources for tapping into the wealth of information proffered by government resources.

http://www.psr.keele.ac.uk

Professor Richard Kimber, retired member of the Department of Political Science, University of Keele, U.K., maintains this very well articulated site. As one might imagine it, is strongest on British politics, but it does have remarkable breadth and is far from parochial.

The homepage is divided into eighteen separate categories, including *Area Studies, Official Government Pages, Constitutions, Treaties and Official Declarations, Elections and Electoral Systems, Political Thought, International relations*, and *Data archives*. Each category lists dozens of the top sites in the field. For instance, under *Area Studies* one finds an alphabetic directory of nations and related sites ranging from Albania to Zimbabwe. There is equally extensive international coverage located under the categories of *Official government pages*, and *Elections and Electoral Systems*. In the volatile world of politics what gives Professor Kimber's work special value is his devotion to maintaining the currency of the site, which is frequently updated on a weekly basis. For a more theoretical and methodological orientation to political science see, Professor Richard Tucker's **Political Science Research Resources** at **http://php.indiana.edu~rmtucker/polssrc.html**. And for more of an emphasis on American politics, see Professor Bob Duval's **Poly-Cy: Internet Resources for Political Science** at **http://www.polsci.wvu.edu/PolyCy/**.

http://www.isn.ethz.ch

This superb site is updated on virtually a daily basis and is maintained by the Center for Security Studies and Conflict Research at Zurich, Switzerland. ISN is elaborately organized and allows multiple avenues to locate information.

The homepage is divided into frames and allows one to either search the entire site or choose among the headings *Subjects*, *Regions*, *Current* (events), *Institutes*, *Conferences*, and so forth. Each of these headings is, in turn, subdivided into multiple categories. For instance, under *Subjects* one finds twenty-one categories, including *International Relations*, *International Law*, *Military/Defense*, *Arms Control*, *Disarmament/Conflict Management*, *Minorities/Ethnicity*, *Human Rights*, *Extremism/Terrorism*, *Environment/Resources*, and many other interesting topics.

A particularly appealing aspect of ISN is that each individual link is furnished with a solid description and that there is a very useful set of icons indicating whether a site is full text, contains statistical data or organizational information, or possesses links to external sites. The category for *Regions* has a similar well-articulated structure that divides the globe into twenty-one distinct geopolitical units, and there is also a search form that enables one to focus on individual nations. Clearly, a great deal of work has gone into the creation of ISN, and it has set a very high standard for other sites in the area. A recent and even more comprehensive site is **The WWW Virtual Library: International Affairs Resources** at **http://www.etown.edu/vl**. If one's interest is late breaking international news try **The Online Intelligence Project** at **http://www.icg.org/intelweb/frame.html**.

Project Vote Smart
http://www.vote-smart.org/

This site backs up the remarkable claim that it tracks the performance of over 13,000 federal and state political leaders. Project Vote Smart is headquartered out of Corvallis, Oregon, and is the major program for the Center for National Independence in Politics. The project

is scrupulously nonpartisan and its membership cuts across the political spectrum to include figures as divergent as Barry Goldwater and George McGovern. In order to insure its impartiality the Project neither endorses candidates or issues, nor accepts funds from government, corporate, or special interest groups or lobbies.

There are several different ways to search the site, but the most basic method is to fill in the zip code query form featured in the middle of the homepage. This retrieves a list of elected officials representing that particular area, including the president, members of the U.S. House and Senate, and the state's local representatives and governor. Clicking on *U.S. Representative*, for example, yields a tremendous amount of information. One is furnished not only with basic biographical data, appointments within the House, and contact information, but there is also a detailed record of sources of campaign funding and voting record.

In addition, there is an extensive performance evaluation by Special Interest Groups, wherein an organization like Planned Parenthood or Christian Coalition ranks individual politicians suitability with their constituency on a scale of 0 to 100. There is also posted a response to a questionnaire designed by the Project (The National Political Awareness Test) that straightforwardly elicits what positive issues candidates support. The overall result is a well-rounded image of the political figure in question.

Other methods of searching the Project are through clicking on *Candidates and Elected Officials* and *Congress Track*. The former offers access to the complete database of elected officials and shows how they stack up with regard to issues, voting records, campaign finance, and so forth. The latter focuses on the legislative track record of the 106th Congress. Here one finds not only the status and full text of legislation, but also roll call votes, committee assignments, congressional agencies, and complete legislative calendar. Finally, there are links to numerous other political sites. Indeed, the modest homepage for Project Vote Smart belies the wealth of information available. If the interest is electoral data and behavior, see the massive **NES: National Election Studies** at **http://www.umich.edu/~nes**.

Political Resources on the Net

http://www.agora.stm.it/politic

Roberto Cicciomessere is the editior of this Italian site focused on elections and political parties throughout the world. Even though there are over 5,800 links the site is easy to navigate and locate information. One can search by either selecting a country's first initial or clicking on a map representing the continents. Each individual nation has buttons representing *Organizations*, *Governments*, *Media*, and *El ections*. Below the buttons there are links to the nation's principal political parties, electoral results, and frequently a few essays explaining that particular electoral system. In addition, Mr. Cicciomessere has assembled a remarkable list of active political parties. For instance, selecting Great Britain one finds the platform of the New Communist Party or the Scottish Nat ional Party. One will also be astonished by the number of fringe parties represented for the United States. The site is updated on virtually a daily basis and offers a convenient means of charting internal political developments throughout the globe.

Institute for Research in Social Science Public Opinion Poll Question Database

IRSS Data Archive

http://www.irss.unc.edu/data_archive/pollsearch.html

This ingenious site is located at the University of North Carolina at Chapel Hill. The IRSS is a huge repository for public opinion polls, including Carolina polls, Louis Harris polls, Southern Polls, and a variety of individual state polls. If one is looking for statistical information on the President's performance or on political issues ranging from abortion to gun control to environmental regulation, then this is an ideal site.

There are numerous other sites that feature public opinion polls, yet they either require a fee or are somewhat complicated and difficult to navigate. The outstanding attribute here is the ease of access to poll questions and results.

The initial page offers a flexible query form that allows the use of "and" and "or" as boolean operators, and allows the search to be restricted by type of poll (for example, one can focus exclusively on Harris polls) or by decade. After completing the form simply click on the search button at the bottom of the page. The yield is a list of poll questions weighted by proximity to the initial query and a statistical breakdown of responses to the question. In addition, one can retrieve an abstract and catalog number for each particular poll. Another more disparate source for survey and poll data is Princeton's **Survey Research Center** at **http://www.princeton.edu/~abelson**. If one seeks to venture into the more formidable area of survey methodology and software see the homepage for the American Political Science Association's **Political Methodology Section** at **http:/polmeth.calpoly.edu/**.

KENNEDY SCHOOL

CASE STUDIES IN PUBLIC POLICY AND MANAGEMENT

http://www.ksg.harvard.edu/caseweb/

This site features Harvard University's John F. Kennedy School of Government and its innovative method of teaching public policy and administration via the in-depth analysis of actual cases.

The idea is very similar to instruction in law, where students inculcate legal procedure through the focus on past cases. However, the odds are much different in the instance of public administration, where there are neither courts or precedents to serve as guides. In any event, the Kennedy School has collected over 1,500 cases pertinent to policy decisions. The individual cases are chosen according to a number of criteria, but the central attribute of almost all the cases is that they raise difficult issues in terms of policy, logic, and ethics. In short, the cases are chosen to test thinking and ingenuity.

One can search the catalog either through

a keyword search or through browsing a highly articulated topical index. The index alone takes up ten pages of text, and the subjects covered range from abortion to workplace safety. Clicking on a topic retrieves one or more pertinent cases, and clicking on a particular case yields a detailed abstract of the case and a list of cross references to related cases. Unlike most other web sites featured here, this is a commercial site, at least to the extent that acquiring the full text of a case requires payment to the Kennedy School. The costs per case are very reasonable (around $2.50) and can be conveniently ordered online. However, even if one is not interested in purchasing the cases full-text, it is nonetheless fascinating to explore the site and investigate the case method of teaching public policy

http://thomas.loc.gov

Thomas is the principle web vehicle for the U.S. Congress. Started in 1995, Thomas serves as an ideal example of what can be accomplished on the Web and offers a range, depth, and currency of information that no other medium can match.

The site is divided into a number of different categories, but the essential aim is to track legislation. At the top of the page, there is a heading for *Congress This Week*, which covers current activities in the House and Senate. In descending order there are headings for *Bills*, *Congressional Record*, *Committee Information*, and *Historical Documents*. The latter is focused primarily on the founding documents of the nation, such as the Declaration of Independence and the Constitution, although it also includes the amendments to the Constitution up to the present. Under the heading *The Legislative Process* there are two excellent essays detailing how laws are introduced and enacted. At the bottom of the page there is a heading for *U.S. Government Internet Resources*, which refers to other congressional internet services (like the General Accounting Office, Government Printing Office, etc.) and

external federal and state governmental links. In addition, there is a sidebar that furnishes a complete directory to the members of the 106th Congress.

Each of the headings offers an abundance of information. For instance, *Bills* furnishes not only the full text of major legislation from 1973s 93rd Congress to the current 106th Congress, but also includes floor actions, legislative history, Congressional Record page references, committees of referral, amendment descriptions, etc. Moreover, there are multiple means of locating legislation either through sponsor or cosponsor official, short, or popular titles or through subject headings. In short, Thomas delivers the goods.

http://www.law.vill.edu/ fed-agency/fedwebloc.html

This exhaustive site is maintained by Kenneth Mortensen for the Villanova Center for Information Law and Policy. There are a number of sites that perform a similar function, but this one is particularly admirable for its clear layout and comprehensiveness.

Ignoring the heading for *Legislative Branch* that is so magnificently covered by Thomas, there are also main headings for the *Federal Judicial Branc; Federal Executive Branch*; *Federal Independent Establishments and Government Corporations*; *Federal Government Consortium; and Quasi-Official Agencies*; *Federal Boards, Commissions, and Committees*; and *Non-Government Federally Related Sites*. Under each of these heading, there is a complete list of related agencies or institutions. For instance, clicking on *Federal Judicial Branch* retrieves links to the *Supreme Court, U.S. Courts of Appeals, Federal Judicial Center*, and so forth. Clicking on *Supreme Court*, in turn, links to the rich depository of full-text Supreme Court decisions at Cornell University, which contains all cases decided since 1990 and also features 300 of the most historically significant decisions. In addition, there are links to other sites that cover retrospectively the Supreme Court back to 1937.

If one selects *Federal Executive Branch,* one can choose among the *White House*, *Office of Management and Budget*, or *Federal Executive Agencies*. Under the latter one finds the *Department of Commerce*, which alone has links to dozens of subdepartments, agencies and databases, such as the *Bureau of Census*, *Economic Development Administration*, the massive *National Trade Data Bank*, *Minority Business Development Agency*, *National Oceanic and Atmospheric Administration*, *National Weather Service*, *Patent and Trademark Office*, and many others. Each of these areas, in turn, is capable of having immense resources, like the Bureau of Census. Moreover, what applies to what is normally considered the low-profile Department of Commerce applies equally well to almost all the other executive departments and agencies. In other words, one could spend hundreds of hours exploring the dense variety of federal web locations. The great advantage of the Federal Web Locator is that it clearly lays out the administrative structure of the federal government and indicates how each agency or unit fits into the overall design.

State and Local Government on the Net

http://www.piperinfo.com/state/ states.html

This site is a public service furnished by the policy-oriented publishing house of Piper Resources. The homepage is simple and straightforward. At the top of the page, states are arranged alphabetically and there is a date indicating the last time a particular state was updated. One of the virtues of the site is that there are frequent updates.

Clicking on a state retrieves whatever governmental bodies in that state have placed on the web. Some states obviously have more information than others, yet there is not a single state that does not have some sort of web presence. For instance, the state of Illinois has been active in promoting the web. There is not only a *State of Illinois* homepage, but there are separate categories for *Statewide Offices*, *Legislative Branch*, *Judicial Branch*, *Executive Branch* (links to thirty-nine separate departments), *Boards and Commissions*, *Regional*, *Counties*, and *Cities* (forty-four links).

There is no claim to be exhaustive here, in that there are not links to the very numerous Chamber of Commerce sites, but rather the focus is on official government sites. However, there are a number of other categories placed below the index of states focused, on such things as multi-state sites, national organizations like the *National Governor's Association*, and a number of links to other web sites featuring state and local government resources. For a more elaborate subject categorization of state and regional resources, see **NASIRE (National Association of State Information Resource Executives): StateSearch** at **http://www.nasire.org/stateSearch/**.

Psychology

Psychology is the academic discipline devoted to the systematic study of human (and frequently animal) behavior and experience. Although psychology as an object of study has a very long history, its roots in the social sciences date back to the nineteenth century. Some approaches to psychology stress intuition and understanding, yet emphasis here will be on empirical studies aimed at achieving objective knowledge. There will also be only token reference to the related, but still distant disciplines of psychiatry and psychoanalysis.

Even with these restrictions, the psychological sciences cover a very broad array of topics, and there are numerous branches to the discipline. For instance, at the base of the discipline there are studies devoted to uncovering the biological bases of behavior and the rigorous study of cognitive processes, such as perception, learning, memory, thinking, and language. At the other end of the spectrum there are numerous fields of applied psychology, such as clinical psychology and industrial and organizational psychology. However, consistent between all of these different fields and approaches to psychology is an overarching aim of explaining and analyzing individual mentalities and behavior within the broad context of the psychological universe.

PsycSite: Science of Psychology Resources
http://stange.simplenet.com/psycsite

This enormous and comprehensive site is the project of Professor Ken Stange of the Psychology Department, Nipissing University, North Bay, Ontario, Canada. The homepage lists a number of categories, including links to software, professional organizations, university psychology departments, a psychology oriented

chat room, and even a research area that invites interested parties to either conduct or participate in psychology experiments.

All of these categories contain potentially useful information, but the heart and mass of the site is located under the heading, *Info Sources for Psychology*. The complete index of resources runs a full twelve pages. There are numerous subdivisions, starting with links to *Psychology Journals on the Net*, which is followed by an alphabetical listing of subfields within the discipline. Professor Stange enumerates thirty such subfields, like *Abnormal Psychology, Artificial Intelligence, Clinical Psychology, Cognitive Psychology, Memory, Neuroscience, Social Psychology, Tests and Measurement*, and so forth. Each of the subfields, in turn, features a carefully selected set of relevant sites. The clear and well-articulated design of PsycSite makes the site exceptionally easy to navigate. For another interesting yet less comprehensive general orientation to psychology, see **Psychology Web Links by Topic** at **http://www.wesleyan.edu/spn/psylinks.htm**.

http://www.neuroguide.com

An understanding of mind and behavior starts with a notion of the functioning of the brain and neural network. This enormous site with over 4,000 links is maintained by Dr. Neil Busis, chief of the Division of Neurology, Shadyside Hospital, Pittsburgh, Pennsylvania. Although Neurosciences on the Internet has a broader focus than psychology, there is a wealth of relevant information here.

The layout of the site is somewhat complex and takes awhile to get accustomed to. In addition, to a local search engine and an elaborate table of contents, there are also clickable sectional divisions including *Recent Additions, Best Bets, Original* (material), *Academic: Clinical, Images, Software, Diseases, Biology*, and so forth. In addition, there is a unique feature dubbed *NeuroRoulette* by which Dr. Busis randomly selects links from the database. This is not a very systematic way to search Neurosciences on the Internet, but it does furnish a good idea of the wide diversity of links. However, for those who have not visited the site previously, I recommend using the table of contents, which does not exactly reproduce the sectional divisions above.

The heart of the site is located under the category *Neurosciences Resources*, which in turn is divided into a number of subcategories. For instance, under *Neuroscience Internet Guides* there are separate divisions for *Neurosciences, Neurology and Neurosurgery, Psychiatry, Psychology, Cognitive Science,* and *Artificial Intelligence*, and there are many cross references to links within other categories. One area that is particularly fascinating in the way it highlights the richness of the web as an informational medium is the section on images. There is access to thousands of images, in particular, graphic shots of brains, including sheep, primates, rats, frogs, flys, and of course human brains. For a spectacular demonstation of the latter, see Harvard Medical School's **Whole Brain Atlas** at **http://www.med. harvard.edu/AANLIB**. For a somewhat simpler site that covers much the same territory look at **Cognitive-Neuroscience Resources** at **http://www.cnbc.cmu.edu/other/homepages. html**.

AI, Cognitive Science and Robotics

http://www.cs.ucl.ac.uk/misc/ai

Research in artificial intelligence and robotics is a natural extension of the so-called cognitive revolution in psychology. In brief, the cognitive paradigm emphasizes the employment of sophisticated modeling techniques in developing explanations for the workings of the mind.

In this regard computers, and especially computer-processing metaphors, play a prominent explanatory role. Computers play a large role in almost all fields of psychology, but one could say they play a determinate role in the above fields. In any case, this very straightforward page was put together by Stephanie Warrick, who is a Research Fellow in Neuro-

psychology at University College London. The homepage is divided into two divisions with four sections a piece. The first, and most significant division, has headings for *Artificial Intelligence, Cognitive Science, Psychology and Linguistics, Neural Networks, Neurosciences, Genetic Programming, and Artificial Life*, and last *Robotics, Agent Modeling and Vision*. Each of these areas presents a straight alphabetized list of links and resources. Many of the links are furnished with a brief two-or-three sentence description of the contents of the site. However, browsing the alphabetized lists does require some patience, in that they are exhaustive and often include over a hundred links.

The second division is more interdisciplinary and less comprehensive, and features headings for *Conference Lists, Organisers and Past Papers, Journals and Publishers, Usenet FAQs,* and *Resource Guides, Bibliographies, and Indices*. Particularly useful are the latter two items in furnishing basic information on complex concepts such as artificial intelligence and providing additional guides for general information on these advanced fields.

http://www.psych.unizh.ch/genpsy/ Ulf/Lab/WebExpPsyLabAnim.html

Experimental psychology lies at the cornerstone of modern psychological science and this handsome site is maintained by Professor Ulf Reips, Department of Psychology, University of Zurich, Switzerland.

Professor Reips presents a series of four elaborate experiments in which we serve as online participants. The first experiment requires a machine capable of reading JAVA and involves the distinction between simulated visual motion in a two-dimensional field as opposed to a three-dimensional field. The test is easy enough, but the layout is complex. The second experiment is a simple test of probabilistic reasoning, yet arriving at the correct answer is no mean feat. The latter two tests are more lengthy and focus on reading and perception.

All of the tests are genuinely engaging and provide at least a glimpse of the procedures and concerns characteristic of experimental psychology. In addition, Professor Reips offers an in depth discussion of the advantages and disadvantages of web experiments. This is followed by a select list of other sites relevant to psychological experiments and surveys. One of the sites not mentioned in the list that is worthy of a close look is the **Internet PsychologyLab** at **http://kahuna.psych.uiuc.edu/ipl**.

Clinical Psychology Resources

http://www.psychologie.uni-bonn. de/kap/links_20.htm

Clinical psychology is an applied field that focuses on the diagnosis and treatment of psychological problems. This impressive site was created by Ralph Ott for the Department of Clinical and Applied Psychology, University of Bonn, Germany.

The site is divided into nine major categories including *What's New, Starting Points, Disorders, Behavioral Medicine, Psychotherapy, Assessment*, and so forth. Each of these categories is further subdivided into a number of sections. For instance, the category devoted to *Disorders* is subdivided into independent sections on *Affective Disorders, Anxiety Disorder, Dissociative Disorder, Eating Disorders, Obsessive Compulsive Disorder, Personality Disorders, Posttraumatic Stress Disorder, Schizophrenia, Sexual Dysfunctions, Somatoform Disorder*, and *Suicide*. Moreover, many of these specific ailments are further subdivided into topical categories such as treatment, diagnosis, research, and so forth. In short, Mr. Ott has dedicated a great deal of attention to developing a superior organization for his site. It is owing to this marvelous design that despite the breadth and comprehensiveness of the site it is very easy to navigate. Two other outstanding sites that are intimately concerned with clinical psychology and psychological health are **Mental Health Net** at **http:// mentalhelp.net** and the U.S. Department of Health and Human Services **National Institute of Mental Health** at **http://www.nimh.nih. gov/index.html**.

Social Psychology Network

http://www.wesleyan.edu/spn/

This site was an offshoot of a course taught by Professor Scott Polus of the Wesleyan Universrsity, Department of Psychology. In the process Professor Polus has contributed something of real value for anyone interested in exploring the field of social psychology.

At the top of the page there is an area entitled *Social Psychology Options*. The core of this area is located under the heading *Social Psychology Topics*, which is further subdivided into a number of categories, including *Prejudice; Discrimination; and Diversity; Psychology of Gender; Cultural Links; Social Influence; Interpersonal Relations; Group Behavior; Violence, Conflict, Negotiation and Peace; Prosocial Behavior*; and *Disciplines Related to Social Psychology*. Each of these subcategories is subdivided into even more specialized areas, and then finally there are the individual links.

It is particularly interesting that many of the links are not directly related to social psychology but rather are sites that furnish primary material for social psychological research. For instance, under the heading, *Prejudice, Discrimination, and Diversity* there is a subcategory for *Racism and Other Race Related Issues*, which includes links to primary material sites such as the *National Association for the Advancement of Colored People* and the *National Civil Rights Museum*. Or to take another example, under the heading of *Social Influence* there is a subcategory for *Cults and Social Control*. Located here are sites that not only discuss the psychological ramifications of cults, but there is also a link to the notorious *Heaven's Gate* cult site. In addition to the sites grouped under the topical category there are also a mass links under headings dedicated to Ph.D. programs in social psychology, homepages of practicing social psychologists, and some interesting online social psychological surveys and experiments. In short, Professor

Polus's rich site demonstrates his broad purview of the field of social psychology.

The Personality Project

http://fas.psych.nwu.edu/ personality.html

This site is devoted to students and researchers in the field of personality theory, and was created by Professor William Revelle, director of the Graduate Program in Psychology, Northwestern University.

The site is divided in two, the first half of which is dubbed *Recommended Readings*. Here Professor Revelle has compiled an extensive and well articulated bibliography of the core literature on personality theory. There are separate sections dedicated to *Journals, Overviews, Biological Approaches, Behavior Genetics of Personality, Psychoanalytic Readings, Personality Taxonomies, Inteligence, Evolutionary Psychology*, and an interesting grab bag grouped under *Other*. In addition, there are independent sections on *Psychometrics and Personality Assessment, Psychological and Educational Statistics*, and citations to recent review articles pertinent to personality theory culled from the *Annual Review of Psychology*. One distinctive aspect of Professor Revelle's work is that citations are not restricted to web sites. Indeed, the majority of readings Professor Revelle recommends are located in traditional print periodical, monographic, and reference works.

The second half of the site is listed under the category *Personal and Other Useful Webpages*. There are a number of different sections including *Personality Research Labs and Researchers, Course Syllabi, Psychological Organizations, Useful Advice for Students*, and so forth. All of the items listed in this second half of the site are posted electronically and are web accessible.

It is interesting to contrast the print and electronic resources. Unquestionably, and this applies to all fields, the print sources are richer and more varied than the electronic. However, it is equally clear that the web environment is attracting a growing legion of prominent researchers, as is instanced by the presence of

Professor Revelle. Although the web is certainly not about to eclipse print literature, it increasingly serves as a powerful complement to traditional modes of scholarly and academic discourse. One area of personality theory that attracts a great deal of both popular and professional interest are psychological tests. A site that links to hundreds of online psychological tests is **Tests, Tests, Tests** at **http://www. queendom.com/tests.html**. One of the better tests aimed at personality profiling is the **Keirsey Temperament Sorter II** at **http:// www.keirsey.com/**.

http://plaza.interport.net/nypsan

http://onlinepsych.com/jungweb

Psychoanalysis and analytical psychology are not generally taught as core components in most psychology departments. Indeed, on many campuses there is a greater likelihood to encounter Freud and Jung in a literature or history course than in a psychology class. What can be said with certainty is that Freud and Jung are two of the towering intellectual figures of the twentieth century, and their avowed purpose was to rethink conventional notions of psychology and mental well-being.

FreudNet is furnished courtesy of the Abraham A. Brill Library, New York Psychoanalytic Institute. The Brill collection is one of the world's largest devoted to psychoanalysis. The site is divided into a number of different categories, the most important of which is *Sigmund Freud on the Internet*. Located here are excerpts from a number of Freud's works and a complete hypertext version of the 1900 translation of *The Interpretation of Dreams*.

There are also a number of original papers and a very interesting discussion of the recent controversy surrounding the mounting of a Freud exhibit at the Library of Congress. Another button worth investigating is titled *Editor's Choice*, which currently features the marvelous multimedia display of the **Sigmund Freud Museum** at **http://freud.t0.or.at**.

Carl Gustav Jung was an acolyte of Freud, and although they parted ways, their mutual concern with the unconscious gained both a commanding presence. JungWeb is an offshoot of the OnlinePsych, which describes itself as a comprehensive information service for professionals and consumers in the mental health field. The site is somewhat haphazardly organized but offers many items of interest including an extensive bibliography of Jungian works currently in print. In addition, there are original articles and links to sites connected with predominant Jungian themes, such as archetypes, dreams and alchemy. One site of particular note is **C.G. Jung, Analytical Psychology, and Culture** at **http://www.cgjung. com/cgjung**.

Sociology

Sociology is the quintessential nineteenth century discipline in that its emergence paralleled the modernization and industrialization of Western society. The discipline can be defined in a number of different ways. At its most grandiose, sociology is the study of society period, yet at a more pragmatic level the discipline attempts to explain and analyze group processes and patterns of interaction.

There are many different schools of sociology, and the discipline is very frayed at the margins. On the other hand, much of contemporary sociology revolves around the theories espoused by the so-called classic sociologists, such as Marx, Weber, and Durkheim. It is the classic sociologists who furnish a common language for the discipline, and this perhaps also explains the preoccupation with methodological questions. Sociology can be prescriptive in the manner it can weigh in for or against certain policy resolutions, yet it is a world away from the clinical psychologist involved in diagnosing and treating a disorder. In short, sociologists will always be several distances removed from their object of study. One of the greatest challenges and virtues of sociology is to employ data and interpretations that help demystify society. In this regard, sociologists restlessly probe many of the more common features of society, such as marriage and family, class and status, labor and industry, so as to reveal how behavior and experience are shaped by living in society.

http://www.pscw.uva.nl/sociosite

This remarkable site is maintained by Albert Benschop of the Sociological Institute, University of Amsterdam, Netherlands. In terms of comprehensiveness, there are few sites that compare, and its scope and utility far exceed the bounds of just sociology.

The main page is divided into twenty-four categories, including *Subject Areas*, *Sociologists*, *Data Archives*, *Research Centers*, *Search Tools*, and so forth. All of the categories have items of interest, yet the two that carry the greatest weight are those devoted to *Subject Areas* and *Sociologists*.

The former is divided into almost eighty distinct headings, which are presented in an alphabetized list starting with *Activism* and concluding with *Youth*. The range of subjects covered is obviously very broad, and Mr. Benschop has been absolutely tireless in accumulating links for each of the subject areas. For instance, clicking on the heading *Family* retrieves a cluster of sites grouped around the subfield *Sociology of the Family and Children*. There are thirty-six links listed, each of which is furnished with a brief, useful description of the contents of the site. In short, it does not take much exploration to appreciate the vast dimensions of SocioSite.

The second major category deals with practicing sociologists. There are links to over fifty classical and contemporary sociologists who are listed alphabetically, starting with Theodor Adorno and concluding with Paul Willis. Most of the formative figures in the discipline are located here, and the materials include complete works, excerpts, commentaries, bibliographies, and even a fully searchable database from the *Marx/Engels Archive*. As mentioned, there are many other categories worth exploring that may not be focused exclusively on sociology such as *General Links* and *Search Tools*, yet are excellent in their own right. The one thing to keep in mind is that if visiting SocioSite, plan to stay for awhile. There are a number of other solid guides to sociology that deserve mention: Professor Michael Kearl's **Sociological Tour Through Cyberspace** at **http://www.trinity.edu/ ~mkearl** and **Sociology Internet Resources** at **http://www.wcsu.ctstateu.edu/socialsci/socres.html**.

Dead Sociologists' Society

http://www.runet.edu/~lridener/ DSS/DEADSOC.HTML

This site is the creation of Professor Larry Ridener, Radford University. Professor Ridener has assembled what is in effect a textbook profiling the careers and works of the classic sociologists. The sixteen figures are listed in rough chronological order, starting with *Comte,* then *Martineau, Marx, Spencer, Durkheim, Simmel, Weber, Veblen, Addams, Cooley, Mead, Park, Thomas, DuBois, Pareto,* and *Sorokin.*

If the site is conceived of as a book, each of the sociologists is accorded their own individual chapter. Typically, a chapter is headed by a graphic of the featured sociologist followed by a substantial and detailed portrait of the figure's life and career, and then a careful assesment of their ideas. The great bulk of the text (with the exception of Martineau, Addams, and DuBois) was lifted from Lewis Coser's excellent 1977 survey, *Masters of Sociological Thought:Ideas in Historical and Social Context,* and the graphics were copied from Don Martindale's 1960 publication, *The Nature and Types of Sociological Theory.* In addition, each of the chapters is graced with an individual work of the sociolgist under discussion. For instance, the chapter on Simmel concludes with the marvelous essays, *The Stranger* and *Conflict as Sociation.* At the tail of the homepage Professor Ridener has also furnished a solid general outline and links to subfields within sociology. In this regard the site as a whole offers a first rate introduction to sociology and sociological thinking.

Family Relations

http://www.personal.psu.edu/ faculty/n/x/nxd10/family3.htm

Families and kinship networks furnish the core components of social organization. This ingenious site is the upshot of an upper-dvision course in family relationships taught by Professor Nancy Darling of the Department of Human Development and Family Studies, Penn State University.

The site is divided into five large sections, *Relationships*; *Parenting*; *Grandparents and Brother/Sister Relationships*; *Family problems*;

and *Intimate violence.* Each of these large sections is divided into subsections, such that *Relationships* is subdivided into *Dating and Sexuality, Communication, Living as Partners, Breaking Up,* and *Not All People Are Straight.* The subsections, in turn, are subdivided into a number of mini-essays addressing different aspects of the topic at hand. For instance, the section on *Dating and Sexuality* has headings for *Are There Sex Differences in Dating?*; *Personal Striving: Different Dating Strategies Used by Men and Women*; *What* Happens *on a Date,* and so forth.

What is particularly impressive is that Professor Darling recruited her students to author all of the mini-essays, which are of a uniformly high order. The mini-essays are usually short and to the point, and have an attached bibliography. The cumulative effect is that Professor Darling's students have produced a noteworthy and polished textbook on family relationships. In addition, to the five main components of the text the homepage also has an area dedicated to external links for family relationships. The one limitation of "Family Relations" is that it is almost exclusively focused on the contemporary, and usually Caucasian, American family. For a broader perspective accenting the diversity of familial relationships see the tutorial addressed to **Kinship and Social Organization** at **http://www.umanitoba.ca/ faculties/arts/anthropology/kintitle.html**.

http://www.uiowa.edu/~grpproc

The director of the Center for the Study of Group Processes is Professor Barry Markovsky, Department of Sociology, University of Iowa. The Center is highly interdisciplinary, but as the title indicates the fundamental focus is on analyzing the principles by which groups behave and act in society. The units of analysis range from the family to large formal organizations, such as political parties and corporations. There is an equally strong emphasis on theory and the application of innovative research methods, especially computer-related applications. In short, the Center stands at the cutting edge of research on social groups.

The site is divided into a number of sections, the two most significant of which are the Center's own electronic journal, *Current Research in Social Psychology*, and *Links to Web Sites of Related Interest*. The journal is currently in its fourth year of publication and is peer reviewed.

The second area dedicated to related links lists twenty separate sites. Many of the links are of a general nature, yet there are also some outstanding examples of current research. For instance, there are links to Professor Peter Burke, Washington State University, who developed the influential idea of identity theory and has been a pioneer in programming comcomputer simulations of social behavior. And Professor David Heise, Indiana University, who has made available some sophisticated online experiments analyzing social interaction. In additon, there is a link to the *International Network for Social Network Analysis*, which connects to its journal *Connections*, and a number of very interesting sites that offer computer generated graphical representations of complex social networks and interactions.

Links to Activism Sites on the Web

http://www.u.arizona.edu/ ~nvandyke/active.htm

This site is an offshoot of the section devoted to Collective Behavior and Social Movements of the American Sociological Association. Activists are an essential component of social movements, and this site functions as an index to the bewildering array of activist groups and causes present on the web.

The activist sites are grouped in broad categories and listed alphabetically, including *African Descent, Anarchy, Conservative, Environment, Farther Right, Human Rights, LesBi-Gay, Libertarian, Nonviolence, Vegetarian, Women, Misc./General/Uncategorized*, and so forth. There is no claim for comprehensiveness, but there is plenty of fodder for any paper focused on social movements. A few examples will suffice. The *Pat Buchanan for President* page has the unique status of fitting under both

the *Conservative* and *Farther Right* categories. The latter also contains the most outspoken hate groups. Environmental groups are well represented including some less familiar organizations such as the *Solar Cooking Archive*. Under the category of *Human Rights* there is the excellent *Amnesty International Home Page*, which offers an extensive library documenting human rights abuses throughout the globe. At the other end of the spectrum, under the category of *Misc./General/Uncategorized* is *Hyperfuzzy* which is a bizarre concoction of cyber-religion with additional links to T. S. Eliot, Timothy Leary, and photos of Crosley cars. One general problem with the activism links is that they need better maintenance and updating. An additional site that opens the door to numerous left leaning social movements and organizations is the **Institute for Global Communications** at **http://www.igc.org/igc/**.

http://www.unicef.org/pon99

This site comes courtesy of the United Nations Childrens Fund and offers a compelling exercise in comparative sociology. The Progress of Nations is an annual report on the health of nations. In doing so the report includes both independent essays and statistical surveys grouped around broad indicators of social health, including *Water and Sanitation, Nutrition, Health, Education, Women, Special Protections, Industrialized Countries*, and *Statistical Tables*.

In each section much of the focus necessarily is on the widespread poverty throughout the globe, and the staggering disparities in the social health of industrialized nations as compared to developing nations. Perhaps even more revealing are the occasional enormous gaps between developing nations. For instance, under the category of *Education,* it is revealed that among the poorer nations Ethiopia, Haiti, Mali and Niger enroll less than 30% of primary age school children, yet Bangladesh, Kenya, Malawi, and Viet Nam with comparable income levels enroll over 80% of primary age school children.

The most telling indicators are listed under the category of *Statistical Tables*. The section *Statistical Profiles* charts 149 nations according to ten criteria, including total population, annual number of births, under-five mortality rate, gross national product per capita, primary school enrollment, maternal mortality rate, and so forth. A glaring example of the chasm between nations is that Switzerland ranks at the top of the GNP with a figure of $40,630, whereas Mozambique ranks at the bottom with a pitiful GNP of $80. These statistics set in stark relief the vast challenges ahead. For additional resources focused on stratification and inequality see **Inequality in America** at **http://epn.org/prospect/inequity.html**, and the massive **Institute for Research on Poverty** at **http://www.ssc.wisc.edu/irp**.

http://www.criminology.fsu.edu/cj.html

Crime and deviance in general have long been mainstays of sociological research, and this comprehensive site is the creation of Dr. Cecil Greek, School of Criminology and Criminal Justice, Florida State University.

Dr. Greek views crime through a wide-angle lens, and the site is divided into sixteen broad categories, including *Federal Criminal Justice Agencies*; *International Criminal Justice Sources*; *Criminal Justice Information*; *Crime and Crime Prevention Pages*; *Juvenile Delinquency and Juvenile Justice*; *Drug and Alcohol Information*; *Police Agencies and Resources*; *The Courts: Due Process and Civil Liberties*; *Pornography, Obscenity, Censorship & The Communications Decency Act*; and so forth. Each of the categories is generally subdivided into more specific headings, and then the individual links are often furnished with a brief description of their contents. For instance, the site's most extensive section, *Crime and Crime Prevention Pages* runs a full twenty-one pages and incorporates thirteen headings, including *Criminal Violence*; *Guns*; *Crime Prevention and Victims Organizations*; *Militias*;

Cults; *Bombers, & Arsonists*; *Organized Crime*; *Computer Crimes*; *Victimless Crimes: Prostitution, Pornography, and Gambling*; the very aptly named *Abnormal Behavior*, and so forth.

The broad categories and their subdivisions allow for easy navigation of the site, yet even more impressive are the range and types of resources available. There are databases, original research and opinion papers, and hundreds of links to remote sites. This breadth of vision is equally evident in the ideological range of resources, such that under the category *Victimless Crimes* one finds the *Heidi Fleiss Home Page* juxtaposed with the *Christian Coalition*. In short, Dr. Greek's page offers a wealth of information for those seeking to explore the subterranean side of society.

Qualitative Research Resources on the Internet

http://www.nova.edu/ssss/QR/qualres.html

Quantitative methods and statistics have dominated sociology and the social sciences in general since the 1950s. In the last decade there has been in certain quarters a general reasssssment. This rethinking of method does not so much question the utility of quantitative information but rather asks whether there are not other techniques of data collection that are equally valid and, indeed, work to broaden the entire research landscape. The upshot has been the qualitative research movement, which has reincorporated such techniques as ethnography, textual interpretation, historical, gender and ethnic studies into a new and more broadly interpretive social sciences methodology.

The current page under review is maintaineded by Dean Ron Chenail of the School of Social and Systemic Studies, Nova Southeastern University. The site design is simple and direct, and the most significant categories are *Web Pages*, *Papers and Other Textual Sources*, *Syllabi*, and an electronic journal edited by Dean Chenail, *The Qualitative Report*. Under each category items are listed in straight alphabetical order by title, and there are not any accompanying descriptive notes. Moreover, the lists of sites are extensive and impressive. For instance, the list of titles under the category *Papers and Other Textual Sources* runs a full twenty-nine pages in length. In short, Dean Chenail has been tireless in collecting materials. On the other hand, navigating the site requires a good deal of browsing and patience. Despite the lack of a sophisticated layout, the site does well convey the tremendous diversity and vitality in the field of qualitative research. A particularly intriguing aspect of qualitative research is its reconsideration of the active and participatory role of the researcher in conducting research. An excellent site tha t discusses these issues and offers examples of completed research is **PARnet: The Cornell Participatory Action Research Network** at **http://www.parnet.org**.

Cybersoc: Sociological and Ethnographic Study of Cyberspace

http://www.socio.demon.co.uk/ home.html

This attractive and well designed site stakes out a newly emerging field of research: the sociology of Internet communities. It is the creation of Robin Hamman, Ph.D. candidate at the Hypermedia Research Center, University of Westminster, U.K.

Much of the site serves as a platform to introduce Mr. Hamman's own work and ideas. For instance, at the top of the page is the full text of Hamman's master's thesis, *Cyborgams: Cybersex Amongst Multiple-Selves and Cyborgs in the Narrow-Bandwidth Space of America Online Chat Rooms*. In addition, there are sections devoted to his current research, a set of personally compiled bibliographies, and even an online journal founded and edited by Hamman, *Cybersociology: Magazine for the Social-Scientific Study of Cyberspace*.

Outside self-promotion, there are also links to remote sources that offer a comprehensive view of the sociology of Internet communities. *Other Papers and the Cybersoc Library* presents dozens of papers focused on online communities and social interaction on the Internet. More engaging yet is the section *Links and Search Tips*, in which Hamman furnishes a step-by-step outline of locating resources on online communities via the world wide web. Cumulatively, the site makes clear that there are many and diverse social implications involved in the advent of the Internet.

Humanities

A common cliché is that in the academic world the humanities are most closely identified with the ivory tower and, hence the most removed from contemporary developments, especially those related to technological advances. In this light one might assume that humanities disciplines would be slow in recognizing the significance and value of the web and the Internet for humanities research. Quite the contrary, numerous humanities researchers have been in the forefront of placing materials on the web and in advocating the Internet as a powerful means of scholarly communication. Indeed, some of the most spectacular sites on the web are humanities-based. In this chapter the focus will be on those sites that attempt to treat the entire range of the humanities. Some of the selected sites may fall more heavily upon one area of the humanities than another, but all of them are notable for their multidisciplinary outlook. If one's primary orientation is toward the humanities, then the sites below offer both a focused view of the web while also bestowing a broad range of choices.

Voice of the Shuttle: Web Page for Humanities Research
http://humanitas.ucsb.edu

This handsome and comprehensive site is the creation of Professor Alan Liu, Department of English,University of California,Santa Barbara. The site is organized around some forty-plus subject headings. As is proper in this interdisciplinary age, Professor Liu inserts a number of headings not traditionally associated with the humanities, such as *Anthropology*, *Cyberculture*, *Legal Studies*, and what he dubs *Postindustrial Business Theory*. More conventional

humanities subject areas, include *Art & Art History*, *Classical Studies*, *Linguistics*, *Literature*, *Literary Theory*, *Music & Dance*, *Philosophy*, *Religious Studies*, and so forth. In addition, there are some general academic categories for locating libraries and university homepages and departments, and various loose links to fun stuff, kid stuff, and Internet navigation stuff.

Each of the subject areas has a very useful *Highlights* section that pinpoints six to ten of the most prominent sites in the field. The organization of the subject areas proper can be quite sophisticated. For instance, the philosophy page is subdivided into ten sections, including *General Philosophy Resources*, *PhilosophicalFields-Aesthetics-Ethics-Logic-Metaphysics-Philosophy of Science-Philosophy of Technology*, *Modern Philosophical Movements-Existentialism-Phenomenology*, *Philosophers & Works*, and so forth. Each section presents an alphabetized series of links, of which many have an attached note describing the source. All tolled, the philosophy page is twenty-three pages in length, and this is not untypical of the other subject areas treated by Professor Liu. In short, the site as a whole is massive.

Another characteristic of The Voice of the Shuttle is the strong presence of post-modernist thought and idioms. This is particularly evident in the sections devoted to *Postindustrial Business Theory* and *Cyberculture*, yet the echo is equally conspicuous throughout. By his own example, Professor Liu reminds us that academic humanities departments are the primary bastion of today's postmodernist thought. There will be repeated reminders of this in the course of navigating the humanities disciplines.

http://www.spaceless.com/hub/

This is another impressive general humanities

site that reaches somewhat beyond the humanities. It originated at the Faculty of Arts, Griffith University, Brisbane, Australia, and now has taken on a life of its own. It is not as comprehensive as some other resources in the field and is strongly biased toward Australian sources, yet it has unique features that deserve mention.

For starters, the subject categories (there are thirty of them, ranging from *Anthropology* to *Women*) are located under a neat pop-up menu on the main page. Clicking on an individual subject category retrieves a set of links, each of which is furnished with a detailed description of the contents of the resource. The category *Art* retrieves thirty-three resources, the category *Literature & Literary Studies* twenty-nine matches, whereas *Philosophy* retrieves sixty-three matches. These are fairly modest numbers, but there are subject areas unique to Humanities Hub. For instance, there is the previously unencountered category of *Kibble*, which to my best reckoning is comprised of bits and pieces. In any case, there is a melange of sites listed here, including the bizarre and wondrous *Postmodern Essay Generator*. This site is a send-up of postmodernism, in that it is comprised of a piece of software entitled the *Dada Engine* that generates text (exclusively drawn from postmodernist jargon) from recursive grammars. Each time the generator is clicked it spits out a new and outrageous essay. My last trip to the site produced the ponderous title, *Deconstructing Baudrillard: Lyotardean Narrative in the Works of Rushdie*. The essays are fully equipped with fictitious authors (often from distinguished universities) and also boast a full bibliography of equally nonsensical titles. This is a small sample of the pleasures offered by the Humanities Hub, which always furnishes unique items of interest.

HUMBUL

HUManities BULletin Board
http://users.ox.ac.uk/~humbul

Emanating from Oxford University, this site certainly has a distinguished pedigree. Started in the mid-1980s as a vehicle for notifying

humanities researchers of upcoming conferences it has evolved into a handsome web site.

HUMBUL is divided into eighteen subject areas, including *Classics*; *Electronic Text Resources*; *Film; Drama & Media Studies*; *Humanities Computing*; *Hypermedia*; *Languages & Linguistics*; *Literature*; *Music*; *Visual Arts*; and so forth. This is by no measure a comprehensive site, but rather is extremely selective. For instance, under the category of *Film, Drama & Media Studies* there are only twenty-two links, whereas the list of potential candidates numbers in the hundreds. A particularly nice feature is that just below each link, there is a button dubbed *Details*, which offers a detailed description of the site in question. Unfortunately, at present only a minority of the links have been furnished with descriptions, and it is hoped that as work advances more contents descriptions will be made available.

There are also buttons for reading comments of other viewers who have visited a site, and it is also possible to add one's own comments. Yet here too these capabilities are largely underutilized. In summary, if you do not want to be overwhelmed with long lists of links and are attracted to the idea of an English slant on humanities resources then HUMBUL may be just the thing for you.

CETH: Center for Electronic Texts in the Humanities
http://sc01.rutgers.edu/ceth/

The advent of the web has intensified the question of what constitutes an authoritative text. The aim of the Center is to aid students and scholars in accessing and implementing projects employing electronic texts by establishing appropriate guidelines Moreover, there is a concern with not only the distribution of texts but also with what computers and the web can contribute to the field of textual analysis.

The site is divided into a number of different categories, including *Introductory Material*, *Information Services*, *Programs*, and

Projects & Prototypes. The introductory section broaches fundamental issues of where to locate electronic texts and how to evaluate them. The section on *Information Services* has a *Directory of E-Text Centers*, which furnishes an alphabetized list of American and foreign universities involved in the dissemination of electronic texts. In addition, there is a lengthy *Humanities Computing Bibliography* that addresses issues ranging from online finding aids to methological issues involving computerized concordancing and text analysis.

The most exciting section features the Center's own *Projects & Prototypes,* including experimental text encoding projects of works by Walter Pater; Zora Neale Hurston; John Donne; Sigmund Freud; the massive *Or lando Project* aimed at women's writings from the British Isles; the marvelous *Model Editions Partnership* focused on historical American documents; and numerous other projects. The site's one drawback is that it has only been sporadically updated, which is a pity considering the increasingly prominent role of electronic textual distribution and analysis for humanities scholarship.

Institute for
ADVANCED TECHNOLOGY
in the
ꤛꤢꤰ꤮ANITIES

IATH: Institute for Advanced Technology in the Humanities
http://jefferson.village.virginia.edu/ home.html

The express goal of the Institute is to "explore and expand the potential of information technology as a tool for humanities research." Located at the University of Virigina, this site well lives up to its name through its presentation of cutting-edge humanities research pro-

jects. What is most impressive is the expansive notion of the humanities promoted here in projects ranging from classical studies to local historical studies of Virginia counties.

The site is divided into six main sections *What's New at IATH*; *Interact with the Institute*; *Reports, Projects, and Works in Progress*; *Postmodern Culture*; *Related Readings in the Humanities*; and *Software*. The first two categories present general information about the Institute and its resources, whereas the latter sections focus on specific humanities projects or theoretical discussions of what information technology holds for humanities research. For instance, under the *Reports* section there is both a beautiful web essay by David Gants, "*A Digital Catalogue of Watermarks and Type Ornaments Used by William Stansby in the Printing of the Workes of Benjamin Jonson (London: 1616),*" and a fine discussion by Hoyt N. Duggan, "*Some Un-Revolutionary Aspects of Computer Editing.*" In addition, IATH is one of the principal supports for the journal *Postmodern Culture*, which was one of the first and still one of the liveliest peer-reviewed journals to appear on the web. The journal has a beautiful layout and each issue features a wide variety of articles and reviews. Be forwarned, however, that the argot and perspective is thoroughly postmodern. For those unfamiliar with pomo speech and thought, the journal serves as an excellent primer. The section *Related Readings* highlights digital humanities initiatives and resources in more than fifty subject areas. The final section devoted to *Software* features programs developed at IATH for incorporating text, audio and graphic data into web pages. It is manifestly clear after visiting this site that the web and the advance of information technologies pose no threat to the humanities, but rather open the door to whole new realms of activity.

Art

This chapter is somewhat narrower than the name implies, in that the focus is restricted to the fine arts or visual arts. Moreover, the primary focus will be on Western culture, although not exclusively so. Even within these confines, however, the visual arts incorporate a broad array of disciplines, including painting and drawing, sculpture, ceramics, photography, architecture, mixed media, and a variety of applied arts.

The web boasts a stunning assortment of fine art sites and innumerable individual artists. The graphic capabilities of the web have obviously opened new ways of displaying and accessing art. On the other hand, viewing scanned images through a fifteen or seventeen inch screen poses serious limitations to the appreciation of individual art works. Despite the drawbacks, a growing number of artists, curators and scholars have ventured to present their works and collections on the web. The web has a flexibility that allows for juxtaposition of works in unique ways and in addition permits a commentary on works that is rare for a conventional museum or gallery.

ART HISTORY RESOURCES ON THE WEB

http://witcombe.bcpw.sbc.edu/ ARTHLinks.html

This grand and comprehensive site is the creation of Professor Chris Witcombe, Department of Art History, Sweet Briar College, Virginia. The site is fashioned in the manner of a textbook with six main divisions: *Part 1, Prehistoric, Ancient and Middle Ages*; *Part 2, Renaissance, Baroque, & Eighteenth-Century Art*; *Part 3, Nineteenth-Century Art and Twentieth-Century Art*; *Part 4, Non-European Art*; *Part 5, Research Resources in Art History*; and *Part 6, Museums and Galleries*.

Each of the divisions is further organized into a number of categories, topics, and individual artists. For instance, the *Renaissance* section contains a fascinating discussion of *The Art of Renaissance Science*. The topics addressed, include Galileo and perspective, human anatomy, the engineering challenges posed by Renaissance architecture, and so forth. Keep in mind this is only a small fraction of a large division, the index of which alone runs more than sixteen pages.

The one division devoted to non-Western art has a good representation and commentary on Asian, and native African, Oceanian, and American arts. The *Research Resources* is a fine compendium of other web image banks and indices of the visual arts, and also contains sections on prints, research methods, and other miscellaneous items. Finally, the section on *Museums and Galleries* offers a marvelous global tour of outstanding art collections. An additional virtue of the site is that it is frequently updated. Professor Witcombe has done himself proud in amassing and meticulously organizing a site of such rich and multiform content.

Louvre Museum
http://mistral.culture.fr/louvre

Museums serve many purposes, but certainly one of their primary functions is to house and display masterpieces of art. Professor Witcombe's section on museums makes it clear that virtually all of the major national museums have some type of web presence, and yet if one museum stands alone, it is Paris' Louvre.

The Louvre was the palace of the French monarchy, and the original structure dates back more than eight hundred years. It was inaugurated as the Louvre Museum at the time of the French Revolution in 1793. The web site is the Louvre's latest incarnation and is available in English in addition to French, Spanish and Japanese. The site is divided into ten sections the most significant of which are *The Louvre*

Palace and Museum, Renovations of the Grande Louvre, The Collections, and *Temporary Exhibitions.* The site is not meant to serve as an exhaustive display of the museum's contents but rather entices the visitor by furnishing an overview of the collection's extraordinary scope, ranging from 6000 BC to the 1850s.

The first two sections, devoted to the physical space of the Louvre offer a detailed history of the palace and its continued evolution. Under *Collections* there are seven de-departments: *Oriental Antiquities and Islamic Art*; *Egyptian Antiquities*; *Greek, Etruscan and Roman Antiquities*; *Objets d'Art*; *Sculptures*; *Prints and Drawings*; and *Paintings.* Each department is topically subdivided with a display of the subdivision's major works accompanied by a brief explanation of the formation of the collection. For instance, the *Department of Paintings* chronologically encompasses the medieval period to the mid-nineteenth century and is subdivided into the *French School, Italian School, Flemish, Dutch and German Schools,* and the *Spanish and English Schools.* The masterpieces on display number only five to nine items per national school, but they nonetheless powerfully convey the Louvre's depth and richness. The *Temporary Exhibitions,* which generally run a year, equally underscore the grand and protean character of the Louvre.

http://www.moma.org

MOMA is dedicated to art produced from the late nineteenth century on, and in this regard its collection begins where the Louvre leaves off. Like the Louvre, MOMA displays very few images compared to its overall collection, yet the masterpieces on view are stunning.

The site is divided into two halves: *Collections* and *Exhibitions. Collections* has separate divisions for *Painting and Sculpture, Drawings, Prints and Illustrated Books, Architecture and Design, Photography,* and *Film and Video.* Each of the divisions is furnished with a brief description of the size and scope of the collection and is accompanied by outstanding examples of the permanent collection. *Exhibitions,* on the other hand, is devoted to programs, events and temporary exhibits sponsored by MOMA. The latter have their own handsome web displays and explanations of the varied exhibits. Another interesting and useful set of external links focused on modern art is located under *Research Resources.* As mentioned above, there are hundreds of fine arts museums accessible from the web. The Louvre and MOMA are merely fine examples. A final similarity is that what these sites do not say directly, yet very effectively convey, is that the digitized image is no substitute for the work of art in its full dimensions.

http://www.saumag.edu/art/studio/ chalkboard.html

We segue here from the ethereal heights of the world's great museums to nuts and bolts instruction on creating art, specifically drawing and painting. This eminently practical and well-executed site is the work of Professor Ralph Larmann, Department of Art, Southern Arkansas University.

The studio is divided into three main units: *Drawing: Perspective, Shading, and Composition*; *Painting: Color Theory, Materials and Techniques*; and *Sources and Resources: Bibliography and Links.* The drawing and painting units are organized like textbooks and are premised on step-by-step acquisition of fundamental skills. For instance, the drawing unit is divided into sections on *Linear Perspective, Atmospheric Perspective, Shading (Value),* and *Compositional Models.* Each of the sections in turn is subdivided into particular aspects of the craft. Moreover, specific skills are graphically represented and then often illustrated with a classic work of art. Three point perspective is thus illuminated by a link to M.C. Escher's

Relativity. The last unit devoted to resources and external web links is modest but does introduce a number of interesting sites focused on art education. For those who want to move beyond art appreciation to the technical aspects of creating works, the Art Studio Chalkboard is an ideal launching point.

Architecture: World Wide Web Virtual Library

http://www.clr.toronto.edu:1080/ VIRTUALLIB/2arch.html

This comprehensive site is the work of Professor Rodney Hoinkes, School of Architecture and Landscape Architecture, University of Toronto. The site is more concerned with architecture as a profession as opposed to an art, but then as with many applied arts, it is difficult to make a sharp distinction between the two. In any case, the site has over 2,300 links, and consequently there is a wealth of material to fit virtually anyone's interests.

The site is divided into six different categories, including *Groups, Individuals, Sources*, and *Talk*. *Groups* is a directory of job listings, professional associations, academic departments, and the like, whereas *Individuals* is primarily oriented toward posting architectural students portfolios on the web. The portfolios come from every corner of the globe, and many are quite elaborate. *Talk* is devoted to news, conferences, and competitions in the field. However, the largest and most significant category is grouped under *Sources*. There are all kinds of things gathered under the category, including professional publications, architectural modeling software, construction materials suppliers, but the most interesting items from an aesthetic point of view are located under the headings of *History* and *Projects*.

The former heading lists approximately seventy-five sites devoted to different aspects of architectural history ranging from the Vatican to the so-called American Prairie School. In addition, *Projects* has a huge amount of diverse material, the vast majority of which could be classified as art historical. The index to this heading alone runs more than twenty-five pages. Owing to the expanse of this section it is subdivided into a number of subsections, including *Architectural Types, Architects, Architectural Sites, Architect's Projects*, and *Imagery Archives*. The precise meaning and significance of each of these subsections is sometimes obscure, but in any case it is here that one finds a full array of geographic architectural types and genres, and it also here that one can locate great architects of the past such as Brunelleschi and Frank Lloyd Wright. Fortunately, if one has a specific interest there is a form to search the entire site placed at the center of the main page. A single caveat regarding Professor Hoinkes' work is that although he has been very diligent in adding new materials, too many of the links listed are no longer operational and should be removed.

http://art.sdsu.edu/ceramicsweb/

This site was created by Professor Richard Burkett, School of Art, San Diego State University. The frames version of the site best reveals its organization, which includes nineteen major headings such as *Class Materials, Articles on Ceramics, GlazeBase Project, Materials Database, Health and Safety, Ceramics Software, Ceramics Info Sites, Potter's Homepages, Museums/Exhibitions*, and so forth.

As is evidenced by the headings the primary orientation is toward the student and practitioner. For instance, *Class Materials* furnishes basic information on creating ceramics, whereas the *GlazeBase Project* is an ambitious attempt to compile an international database of glaze recipes. There is also a great deal of information on the technical aspects of ceramics production, ranging from safety issues (which play a very important role) to the latest software. On the other hand, there is an impressive amount of finished works on display via museums, galleries, and individual potters' homepages. The Ceramics Web is updated on a timely basis and reveals many aspects of the art of ceramics. A large site with a more strictly commercial bent on ceramics is the **WWW Virtual Library: Ceramics** at **http://www. ikts.fhg.ed/VL.ceramics.html**. Another beautiful site devoted to ceramics is the **Museum of Ceramic Art at Alfred University** at **http:// nyscc.alfred.edu/mus/mus.html**.

http://www.webcom.com/cityg/ resource/pa/photarch.html

There are a tremendous number of sites devoted to photography on the web, but there is not one that attempts to comprehend the entire web. PhotArchipelago, however, is a nice start.

The site is a highly selective but well organized collection of photographic lore. It is the creation of two devotees of historic photography, William Allen, Art Department, Arkansas State University, and Steve Knoblock founder of the Internet based City Gallery. From the main page clicking on *Charted Courses* retrieves a directory, that includes *Authors & Photography Historians*, *Collections*, *Exhibits*, *Institutions*, *Literature of Photography*, *Organizations*, *Photographers*, and *Research and Archival Resources*. Each of the headings features a set of a dozen to two dozen carefully chosen links. Although the majority of photographs focus on nineteenth century America, there are also images from throughout the globe dating up to the 1950s.

For a scholarly narrative on the rise of photography, see Dr. Robert Leggat's **A History of Photography: From Its Beginnings till the 1920s** at **http://www.kbnet.co.uk/~**

rleggat/photo/index.htm. The site contains a marvelous dictionary of notable photographers, but it suffers from a serious weakness in that it is bereft of images. For contemporary photography there are any number of sites to choose from. One particularly well organized and updated site is Bruno Navarro's **World Wide Web Photography Sites** at **http://hometown. aol.com/BrunoN/www_ photo_sites.htm**. A final matter to keep in mind is that many of the most renowned photographers and photographic museums are reluctant to post their most prized photographs for the very reason that they are so easy to pirate through the medium of the web.

Thais: 1200 Years of Italian Sculpture
http://www.thais.it/scultura

Like photography, there is not a single site that covers sculpture in a comprehensive way. However, Thais is an award-winning Italian site, one section of which is devoted to a marvelous gallery of Italian sculpture. Do not be put off that the site is not in English (except for the brief descriptions accompanying each piece) because there is very little text. Moreover, it is the wealth of sculpture on display that gives the site its true value.

The site is divided into five different periods: Late Roman and Medieval, Gothic, Renaissance, Baroque, and Modern. Barring the Late Roman and Medieval period, where most of the sculptors were anonymous, each of the other sections list the sculptors and their works in alphabetical order. As one might imagine, the section devoted to the Renaissance is the largest by far and includes hundreds of works by such outstanding artists as Bernini, Cellini, Donatello, and Michelangelo. The images and photography of the pieces are uniformly superb. In addition, towards the bottom of the page are links to the many Italian museums that contributed images of sculptures. For a good survey of contemporary sculpture, see the **International Sculpture Center** at **http://www.sculpture.org**. If one's tastes runs more toward metal sculpture see the **Art Metal Project** at **http://wuarchive.wustl.edu/edu/arts/metal/ArtMetal.html**.

Cyber Art Gallery Eindhoven

http://members.brabant.chello.nl/~cage

The web has not only provided a new venue for the display of art, but with the continued advance of computer and imaging technologies it has also encouraged the development of new types and forms of digital art.

This particular site is the work of Rolf Van Gelder of Eindhoven, Netherlands. Mr. Van Gelder is not only an accomplished artist and computer technician but also a tireless tracker of digital art and artists posted on the web. A fair portion of the site is given over to exhibitions of his work, but the great bulk of the site is located under the category of *Cool Art Links*. It is divided into a number of sections, including *Personal Favorites* (21), *Auctions* (31), *Collective & Workshops* (92), *Design* (58), *Galleries* (429), *General* (236), *Magazines* (34), *Museums* (63), *Resources* (85), and *Schools & Universities* (21). The number succeeding each section indicates the number of attached links. Although there is a fair amount of overlap between the sections, the end result is a comprehensive picture of the realm of digital art. Individual sections feature an alphabetized set of links, each of which is furnished with a brief but telling description. There is an astounding range of works from the whimsical to the spiritual, and Mr. Van Gelder's indefatigable sleuthing testifies to the vitality of contemporary art on the web.

Drama and Theater

The above fields in the performing arts have a strong presence on the web. There are not any neat distinctions between the two. Drama here applies more to the literary activity of writing play, and the textual study and analysis of plays. Theater, on the other hand, is more concerned with performance, and the many tasks (direction, casting, costumes, scenery, lighting, etc.) involved in staging a production. Closely related fields such as film, dance, and opera are dealt with in the chapters devoted to Commmunication Studies and Music, respectively. The thread that holds these arts together is that their full realization is premised on the idea of an audience and the role of the performer as an intermediary between the spectator and the creator. The aim of this chapter is to explore the many skills and contributions necessary for launching a production.

ELAC: East Los Angeles College Theatre Arts
http://www.perspicacity.com/ elactheatre/

This rich and well-organized site is maintained by the Theatre Department of East Los Angeles College. The site is divided into two major divisions: *Theaterpedia:The Internet Theatre Library* and *The Writers Workshop*. The latter is an attempt to guide and form a community of aspiring playwrights. Here one finds practical advice on the craft of playwriting and dramatic structure, and also professional outlets and contacts for contests, festivals, theater companies, and so forth. In addition, there is a substantial collection of new plays and mono-

logues, and an open invitation to submit original works.

On the other hand, *Theaterpedia* is oriented toward established or canonical works in the theater repertory. It functions as a database and includes a comprehensive *Subject Index* and separate subindexes devoted to *Playwrights, Plays by Author, Plays by Title, Sources for Play Texts, Theatre People, Theatre Terms* (Glossary), *Theatre Characters*, and so forth. The database comprehends a massive amount of material, ranging from online texts of Aeschylus to links to Ethel Merman. It would be difficult to not find something of interest here. Another fine comprehensive site is Professor Ken McCoy's **a Brief Guide to Internet Resources in Theatre and Performance Arts** at **http://www.stetson.edu/departments/ /csata/thr_guid.html**.

Ancient Greek Theater
http://homer.reed.edu/Theater.html

Any conception of drama, at least in the West, must start with Classical Greece. This solid, unpretentious site affords a congenial introduction to the Greek theatrical heritage and is maintained by Professor Walter Englert, Department of Classics and Humanities, Reed College.

The site is divided into seven distinct topical areas: *Timeline, Origins; Staging an Ancient Greek Play; Greek Theaters; Structure* (tragic narrative structure)*; English and Greek Texts*; and *Bibliography and Links*. The opening sections explain the chronology, setting, distinctive staging,and thematic elements that combined to form Greek drama. The contextual and critical commentary enhances appreciation of Professor Englert's selection of seven outstanding Greek dramas (courtesy of Tufts University's *Perseus Project*): Aeschylus' *Agamemnon*, *Libation Bearers*, and *Eumenides*; Sophocles' *Antigone*, and *Oedipus the King*; Euripides' *Bacchae*; and Aristophanes' *Clouds*. In addition, there is a small set of links to other sites focused on Greek theater and a useful bibliography of print texts.

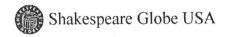 ## Shakespeare Globe USA

http://www.shakespeare.uiuc.edu

Shakespeare remains a dominant literary and theatrical force. As a consequence,the Bard's works possess a vibrant presence on the web with dozens of sites devoted to Shakespeare. One of the best and most comprehensive sites is maintained by Professor Michael Mullin, English Department, University of Illinois at Urbana-Champaign, and Mid-America Education Director, The Shakespeare Globe USA.

Under the heading, *Places to Go* are a number of what Professor Mullin designates as rooms, including *Classrooms* (links to courses and class syllabi), *Design Studio* (stuff on costumes, scenery, and the like), *Playgoers' Room* (annual festivals and productions), *Teachers' Room* (tips for incorporating Shakespeare into the classroom), *Worlds Elsewhere* (international directory of Shakespeare societies and associations), and so forth.

Each of the rooms offer numerous items of interest. However, the most substantial material by far is reserved for *The Library*. It incorporates a number of different sections, the first of which is *The Complete & Individual Works Shelf*. There are links to a variety of online renderings of Shakespeare's works' of which the MIT version is particularly outstanding. Located here are full hypertext versions of all the plays, poems and sonnets, with a glossary and remarkable Shakespeare text search engine. There are additional links to beautiful early editions and facsimiles of the plays. *The Library* also has extensive sections devoted to *Reference* (a broad range of commentary on individual plays and poems, and the general Elizabethan context), *Journals and Articles* (limited to online journals), *The Media Shelf* (Shakespeare on film, television and video), and *The Amusements Shelf* (miscellaneous materials like Shakespearean insults, etc.) All told, Professor Mullin's lovingly assembled Globe offers a fitting tribute to Shakespeare and his works.

http://www.fix.co.jp/kabuki/

We would be remiss to focus exclusively on Western approaches to drama and theater. Many cultures have distinctive and highly developed drama repertoires. As of yet there is not a comprehensive site focused on theater throughout the globe.

In contrast to Western drama, we offer this instructive multimedia site devoted to the traditional Japanese form of theater, Kabuki. The site is the work of Ichimura Manjuro who is himself an actor and authority on Kabuki. Mr. Manjuro's aim is to publicize and introduce the highly stylized and ritualized components of Kabuki to a non-Japanese audience. The site is divided between four major headings: *Online Theater* (frequently updated summaries and video clips of recent plays); *Kabuki Sounds* (Japanese drums and string instruments are an integral part of Kabuki); *Make Up* (a major component of Kabuki character); and *All About Kabuki*. The latter sections contains articles about Kabuki history, plot summaries of some of the major plays, and links to other types of traditional Japanese drama such as Noh and Kyogen. Mr. Manjuro's site allows one to not only appreciate the beauty of Kabuki but also to value its unique cultural distinctiveness.

The Playwriting Seminars

http://www.vcu.edu/artweb/ playwriting

This elaborate and inspired production is the work of Dean Richard Toscan, School of the Arts, Virginia Commonwealth University. The seminar is set up along the lines of a textbook, in which Dean Toscan has identified six key areas for the development of successful playwriting skills.

The skills listed consecutively are: *Content* (stories and themes, character and dialogue); *Film* (screenwritng vs. playwriting); *Structure* (shaping the story); *Working* (writing techniques, rewriting and editing); *Format* (style); and *Business* (submitting scripts, copyright, royalties, etc.). Each of these skills is in turn divided into sections. For instance, the *Content* unit has separate areas devoted to *Characters, Conflict, Settings, Subjects of Plays, Subtext, Themes, Titles,* and *Voice.* In short, it is easy to perceive the textbook structure. On the other hand, there is no need to read the chapters of the work consecutively, and each of the individual sections stands well on its own. Moreover, what really makes the seminar work is the consistently high level of writin, and the numerous examples and quotes from contemmporary playwrights that Dean Toscan incorporates into the text. In addition to the areas devoted to honing playwriting skills, the site also includes a wise selection of *100 Quotes on Craft,* and a highly select *Reading List* of thirty-seven plays to mine for ideas and motivation. For those who want to try their hand at playwriting Dean Toscan furnishes an ideal guide.

Acting Workshop On-Line

AWOL: Acting Workshop On-Line

http://www.execpc.com/~blankda/acting2.html

This fine site is a one-stop resource for inforrmation on the skill and profession of acting.

The site is divided into a number of different areas, including a section of recommended books and readings, an extensive interactive question and answer page, and a well-organized set of hundreds of links that attempts to encompass the many different as-

pects of the trade ranging from training to unions and professional groups.

However, the heart of the site consists of a series of eleven essential lessons for the aspiring actor. The lessons are: *What Every Actor Needs To Know; The Nerves (Stage Fright); "I Gotta Get An Agent!"; Acting As Conversation; Getting Physical; Line! Line! What's My Line?; Auditions Will Be Held For...(a few helpful hints); Help! I Got The Part! Now What?; What About Scams?; Help! I Gotta Get a Monolog!;* and *An Actor's Life.* Each of the lessons reads like an independent chapter, and cumulatively they indicate the many challenges confronting the would-be actor. Make no mistake, the editors of the Workshop do not present a romantic or rosy view of the profession. Although they certainly do not argue against venturing into acting, they make it very clear that only a small percentage of those who enter the profession are able to support themselves exclusively through acting. Hence, there is an equal emphasis on not only the acquisition of skills but also on the business aspects of the profession (incluuding the avoidance of scam artists) and the need to have competent representation through an agent and union. The broad experience of the editors of the Workshop is evident throughout, and it would be wise to closely examine their advice before considering a career in acting.

The Costume Page: Costuming Resources Online

http://users.aol.com/nebula5/costume.html

Costumes and make-up, especially for period pieces, are an integral element of staging a production. This astonishing site is the creation of Ms. Julie Zetterberg of Seattle. Its more than 1,900 links strongly testify to the interest and energy dedicated to costuming.

With this type of volume it is essential that the site be well-organized. Ms. Zetterberg has marshaled her materials by dividing them be-

between twelve main headings. The first five areas are grouped under the general heading *The Study of Costume*, which includes *Reference Works & Museums*, *Costume History*, *Historical Topics*, *Ethnic & Folk Costume*, and *Theatrical Costume*. Each of the headings is divided into a number of subheadings and then each of the links is listed alphabetically under the appropriate subheading. The materials covered range from the ancient world to the present and future, in that there is an extensive store of science fiction costumes. A few examples will suffice to indicate the richness of costuming resources: *Roman Pula: Attire, Footwear, Hairdo*; *Ninth Hussars 1st French Empire*; *The Regency Footwear Page, 1790-1829*; *Women's Undergarments: Past to Present*; *The Turban of the Sikhs*; and so forth.

In addition to the formal study of costumes there are extensive sections grouped under the headings of *Making and Wearing Costumes* and *Sources of Costumes & Accessories*. The former indicates how to learn and get involved in the craft by furnishing a comprehensive list of schools, organizations and associations. There are also detailed instuctions on how to teach yourself costuming. The latter heading focuses on where and how to purchase costuming supplies. To ensure that she has left no stone unturned, Ms. Zetterberg has included an extensive set of related links and a hefty section devoted to Halloween costumes.

The International Theatre Design Archive —Project 2000: 2000 Theatre Designs by the Year 2000
http://www.siue.edu/PROJECT2000

The behind-the-scenes work of stagecraft and design is among the principal underpinnings of theatrical productions. This site serves as a storehouse of ideas for theatre design, and is a spin-off of one of the principal organizations in the field—the United States Institute for Theatre Technology.

The Archive features links to images donated by set designers, costumers, and lighting technicians. The site is divided between three principal headings: *Scene Designs*; *Costume Designs*; and *Lighting Designs*. Each of these headings in turn is searchable by either play title, playwright, designer, or producer. The weakest of the sections deals with costumes, but the topic is so well covered in the site above that it is no great loss. On the other hand, the sections devoted to set and lighting design offer a broad array of playwrights and titles to choose from. A substantial majority of the designers and producers represent university faculty or academic productions, but are certainly no less instructive for that. In any case, the aim of the Archive is not only to aid designers in furnishing a permanent record of their productions but also to assist forthcoming productions by maintaining an online index of professional theatre designs. It is hoped that the archive will achieve its ambitious goal of 2000 links by the year 2000.

Inter-Play: An On-line Index to Plays in Collections, Anthologies, and Periodicals
http://www.portals.org/interplay

Many plays in print, in particular current ones, are not published independently or individually. As a consequence, they are difficult to locate by a conventional author or title search in a library catalog. More often than not plays will appear in collections, anthologies, and periodicals. Although there are several print indexes designed to help locate plays, Robert Westover and Janet Wright, Humanities Libraarians, Portland State University, have devised this ingenious online index. Compiling the database was a massive undertaking, in that it comprises over 15,000 citations and includes languages other than English.

Moreover, despite the density of the database, it is exceptionally easy to search. Simply type in author, title, or both and click on search. The citations matching the search indicate not only the author and title, but also the source, edition, imprint, page numbers and also Portland State's Library of Congress call number. Inter-Play is a marvelous contribution and a tremendous aid in ferreting out plays located in sometimes difficult and out-of-the way places.

English Literature

This chapter focuses on works of imaginative fiction, poetry and criticism. Such a vast and rich body of literature can not be encapsulated in a few sites so stern restrictions must be imposed.

The principal terrain to be covered is what is conventionally referred to as the canon, or those works that through time have proved to have an abiding and enduring interest. In short, we are referring to works of high art. There is certainly not always a sharp distinction between fiction and nonfiction, and specific works of travel fiction, history, or autobiography can certainly be considered legitimate representatives of the canon. Thus, even accepting the restrictions of the canon there are hundred of notable sites illustrating the many genres and forms, historical periods, and literary movements that constitute the evolution of English literature.

Literary Resources on the Net

http://andromeda.rutgers.edu/ ~jlynch/Lit/

The introductory chapter on humanities resources includes some of the best sites devoted to English literature, in particular Professor Alan Liu's outstanding *Voice of the Shuttle.* Of equal note, however, is the meticulously organized and comprehensive site created by Professor Jack Lynch, English Department, Rutgers University, Newark Campus.

A search form is placed at the top of the page, and below follows a set both of chronological and thematic categories. Individual categories, include *Classical & Biblical, Medieval, Renaissance, Eighteenth Century, Romantic, Victorian British, Twentieth-Century British and Irish, American, Theatre and Drama, Theory, Women's Literature & Feminism, Ethnicities & Nationalities, Other National Literatures, Bibliography & History of the Book, Hypertext,* and *Miscellaneous.* As is evident, not all the categories are restricted to English literature, but the site's strength and bulk is clearly focused on English language resources.

For instance, in the huge section devoted to the eighteenth century, British writers dominate the scene, and there are excellent entries ranging from William Blake to Mary Wollstonecraft. The Romantic and Victorian eras enjoy a similarly expansive treatment. Interestingly, American literature is handled as an independent category, and the section is especially strong on contemporary novelists. A number of the remaining categories are notable for their clear postmodernist slant such as the sections on literary theory, women's literature, and ethnicities. The last category devoted to miscellaneous items has valuable leads and information, including sections on *General Guides to Literary Web Resources, Electronic Text Collections,* and a directory of *English Department Homepages.*

Literary Calendar: An Almanac of Literary Information

http://litcal.yasuda-u.ac.jp/

This ingenious site comes courtesy of Yasuda Women's University, Hiroshima, Japan. The coverage is much broader than English literature, yet the majority of individuals represented are English writers. In any case, the site works literally as a calendar of literary events.

Anytime one logs onto the site there appears a quote for the day and a gridded daily calendar for the month. Clicking on a day within the month retrieves a series of notable literary events that mark that particular day. Generally, there will be a series of four or five notable events. There is also a form that allows one to select any month and day of the year. In addition, there is a secondary form that allows searching of the entire site or calendar. For instance, typing in the name Hemingway retrieves eight hits marking the novelist's career from his birth in Niles, Michigan, on June 3, 1885 to his death in Ketchum, Idaho on February 7, 1961. Although the *Literary Calendar* cannot (and does not) make any heavy claims as a scholarly tool, it does demonstrate an inventive, entertaining, and often instructive use of literary lore.

Old English Pages

http://www.georgetown.edu/cball/ oe/old_english.html

This marvelous multimedia site is maintained by Professor Catherine Ball, Department of Linguistics, Georgetown University. It is divided into numerous categories, including *Electronic Texts, Translations & Manuscript Images*; *Art*; *History*; *Language*; *Sound Files*; *Courses*; *Reference*; and so forth.

Each of the categories present items of interest, but in the context of English literature the first category focused on texts, translations, and images is the most germane. Professor Ball has left no stone unturned in seeking out hypertext and web versions of Old English texts and manuscripts. As one might imagine, much of the initial literature in Old English was concerned with the Bible, and there are a number of beautiful examples of books of the Bible and Psalms. In addition, there is a broad variety of epic poetry with numerous links to differing versions of *Beowulf*. Many of the texts are annotated and graced with images of the beautiful original manuscripts. Professor Ball has also furnished telling comments for links to each of the texts.

The remaining categories offer a broad array of information. For instance, the history section helps place Old English literature in context, and located here is a beautifully rendered map of Anglo-Saxon England and links to such notable events as the Battle of Hastings. The language and reference sections offer solid introductions to learning Old English, and the sound files allow one to hear the sound and cadence of spoken Old English. In short, this is an admirable site in every respect. If one's tastes runs more toward Middle English there is a rich collection of annotated texts maintained by **TEAMS (The Consortium for the Teaching of the Middle Ages) Middle English Texts at http://www.calvin.edu/~ksaupe/ teams.html**.

Early Modern Literary Studies

Early Modern Literary Studies: A Journal of Sixteenth- and Seventeenth-Century Literature

http://purl.oclc.org/emls/emlshome. html

This distinguished electronic journal is edited by Professor R. G. Siemens, English Department, University of Alberta, Edmonton. The first issue of the journal was April 1995, and it has since appeared on a regular basis. Most of the articles and reviews would be a tough go for an underclassman, in that they assume a specialized knowledge of the literature and the period. However, there are two general divisions within the site, *Electronic Texts* and *WWW Resources*, that are external to the journal and possess a broad relevance and utility.

The first category offers a diverse range of online texts extending from Francis Bacon to Sir Thomas Wyatt. John Milton, Edmund Spenser and, of course, Shakespeare are particularly well represented. The category on web resources is divided into a number of thematic sections including not only individual writers, but also areas devoted to the art and architecture, history, science, music, philosophy, and religion of the period. The cumulative effect is a very solid grounding in sixteenth- and seventeenth-century English literature.

ROMANTIC CHRONOLOGY

http://humanitas.ucsb.edu/projects/pack/rom-chrono/chrono.htm

The eighteenth century is splendidly represented in the previously mentioned site of Jack Lynch (*Literary Resources on the Net*), and therefore we proceed directly to the romantic era.

This site is maintained by Professor Laura Mandell, Department of English, Miami University, Ohio, and the ubiquitous Alan Liu, Department of English, University of California, Santa Barbara. Profs. Mandell and Liu, perhaps wisely, do not fuss over the contentious topic of the definition of romanticism. What can be said is that they cast a very wide net, indeed. Instead of trying to impose a strict periodization for the movement, they opt to cover a tremendous area of both thematic and chronological ground. For instance, romanticism according to their timeline is divided into twelve separate periods, starting with a very select set of seventeenth century events and concluding with the era 1838-1851. However, the great bulk of the resources fall between the dates of 1785 and 1830, which conforms to more traditional concepts of the romantic movement.

In any case, there are a number of ways the site can be searched. First, one can click on one of the twelve designated time frames, say 1796-1798, and retrieve a strict chronological list of literary texts, and events marking the period. Under 1796-1798 are located approximately seventy events, literary and otherwise. Highlighted text furnishes either internal or external links, or both. For instance, under 1796 there is an entry for *William Wordsworth, The Borderers. A Tragedy.* Clicking on *Wordsworth* retrieves an extensive directory of internal links to Wordsworth, whereas clicking on *The Borderers* retrieves an external link to the full text of the play.

The chronological configuration of the site is oriented toward a leisurely browse. Although there are many fascinating nuggets to be unearthed, browsing is not an efficient method of searching for those who are either in a hurry or have a good idea of what they want. A second method of searching is to click on the category of links archive. Doing so retrieves a pyramid of alphabetized links with a carefully selected set of *General* sites placed at the top. In this manner one can locate William Blake resources by simply clicking on "B" and scrolling down the page to Blake. A search form is also provided as a third means of exploring the site. My recommendation, however, is to forgo the search form at least, in terms of initial contact with the site. No doubt a quick keyword search is very efficient, but to appreciate the scope and magnitude of the project it is best to browse it early on. By this means one gains a much-heightened appreciation of the context of the literature of the period. A very promising site under construction devoted to romanticism is **Romantic Circles** at **http://www.rc.umd.edu**.

Jane Austen Information Page

http://www.pemberley.com/janeinfo/janeinfo.html

There are far too many noteworthy writers in English to post the individual homepages dedicated to them and their works. An exception will be made for Jane Austen, however, because this particular page is such a stunning example of what can be accomplished with the web as an academic resource. The page is maintained by Henry Churchyard, a Ph.D. candidate in Linguistics, University of Texas, Austin.

It is evident from the outset that Mr. Churchyard has devoted countless hours constructing this shrine to Jane Austen. The site is divided into four main divisions: *Jane Austen's writings*; *Jane Austen's life*; *Jane Austen's art*; and *Jane Austen bibliography*. Each of her six mature novels—*Northanger Abbey, Sense and Sensibility, Pride and Prejudice, Mansfield Park, Emma*, and *Persuasion*—are available in full-text along with annotations. Of particular note is a hypertext edition of *Pride and Prejudice* (the other novels are formatted in plain ASCII) with cross-referenced notes and annotations, including a chronology, a list of characters (with full genealogical charts), a list of passages illustrating the motifs of "pride" and "prejudice," a map indicating important places in the novel, notes on random topics, and so forth.

The sections devoted to Austen's life and art are equally well-developed and offer a staggering array of biographical and critical information. In addition, Mr. Churchyard has assembled what he dubs a "selective bibliography," which in actual fact includes hundreds of citations, links, and cross-references. Finally, Mr. Churchyard includes a set of search forms, one of which searches the texts of Jane Austen's novels and the other which searches files within the site. The bibliography and the search forms, like all the other features in the site, are a striking monument to scholarly diligence.

The Victorian Web

http://landow.stg.brown.edu/ victorian/victov.html

This engaging and prestigious site is the work of Professor George P. Landow, English and Art History, Brown University. The site offers a comprehensive examination of the Victorian era, and Professor Landow does not shy away from complexity and offering alternative views of the era.

Literature lies at the heart of the project, and more than thirty writers are featured ranging from Matthew Arnold to Christina Rosetti to Oscar Wilde. The category of *Victorian Literature Overview* has a number of separate divisions, including *Timeline, Authors, Concept of Literary Canon, Literary Techniques, Genres and Modes, Victorian Periodicals*, and *Literary Convergences*. Each of these divisions contains substantial material, but of particular note is the extensive discussion of the hotly contested issue of the process of literary canonization.

The literary cast of the site is supplemented by independent categories devoted to *Social Context, Economics, Religion, Philosophy, Visual Arts, Science, Technology*, and *Gender Matters*. In addition, there is an important category focused on analyzing the meaning of the idea of *Victorianism*. Some of these areas may be of more interest or relevance than others, but each is very well developed with numerous links. One leaves the Victorian Web with a heightened appreciation of what Professor Landow terms "this complex, paradoxical age that was a second English Renaissance."

MODERN

VOICE OF THE SHUTTLE: ENGLISH LITERATURE

http://humanitas.ucsb.edu/shuttle/ eng-mod.html#british

It may appear that there is an over reliance on Professor Alan Liu's Voice of the Shuttle, but the simple fact of the matter is that this site offers the best and most comprehensive coverage of late-nineteenth and twentieth-century British and American Literature.

At the top of the page are listed a number of interesting items under the category of *General Resources*, which discuss the concept of modernism. However, the vast bulk of the guide is divided between alphabetized lists of British and American authors with a strong web presence. The British list includes a wide range of authors, with especially substantial contributions for Auden, Chesterton, Eliot, Aldous Huxley, Joyce, D. H. Lawrence, Virginia Woolf and W. B. Yeats. It should be noted, however, that there are few post-WWII writers on the British side. In this regard, contemporary American literature receives a fuller treatment, with Allen Ginsberg and the "Beat Generation" particularly singled out for notice. There are also solid contributions among others for e.e. cummings, Faulkner, Hemingway, Langston Hughes and the Harlem Renaissance, Vladimir Nabokov, Gertrude Stein and Richard Wright. An interesting chronological approach to twentieth-century literature is located at the **Modernism Timeline, 1890-1940** at **http://faculty.washington.edu/eckman**.

AMERICAN LITERATURE

http://www.keele.ac.uk/depts/as/Literature/amlit.html

In the virtual world, the old adage of staying close to one's own backyard does not always apply. For instance, one of the top sites for American literature is an extension of the American Studies Program at Keele University, U.K.

The site is divided into a number of different categories, including *Special Features* (colloquia and the like on American literary figures hosted by Keele), *Other American Literature Web Sites*, *Teaching Resources*, *Canadian Literature*, and *Global Literature Sites*. However, the bulk and heart of the site is located under the category of *Virtual Libraries*. This category in turn is divided into three major sections: *Mimi, E-Texts and Resources 18th/19th Centuries*; *Sally Anne, E-Texts and Resources, 20th Century*; and *Writing Black, Literature by and on Blacks*. Each of these sections presents an alphabetized list of authors, and their works or other resources, like bibliographies, profiles, and so forth available over the web. Of particular interest is the comprehensive treatment of the rapidly expanding field of African-American Literature. The selection of writers is diverse and eclectic and includes not only novelists and poets, but activists such as W. E. B. DuBois and Malcom

X. For an even larger site that boasts over 700 American authors, see **American Authors on the Web** at **http://www.lang.nagoya-u.ac.jp/%7Ematsuoka/AmeLit.html**.

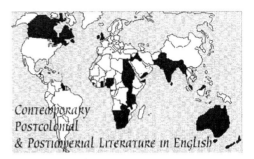

http://landow.stg.brown.edu/post/misc/postov.html

Professor George Landow, renowned for the *Victorian Web*, is also the driving force behind this site. The term and concept of Postcolonial Literature is relatively new and at present is a vigorously growing field.

In the simplest terms Postcolonial English deals with those regions, former colonies, where the English language remains a powerful, if not necessarily dominant, force in literature, governmental and intellectual discourse. Obviously, the emergence from colonial status varies greatly from region to region as, for instance, the dramatic differences between India or Ghana, or Australia and New Zealand. On the other hand, theorists in the field contend there are sufficient common threads among the former colonies to group them under the umbrella term Postcolonial. This site goes a long way in presenting and examining a number of these common threads.

The homepage is divided along both regional and thematic lines and includes categories for *Africa, Australia, India, Caribbean, New Zealand, United Kingdom, Authors* (more than fifty authors are represented), *History, Politics, Religion, PoCo Theory, Bibliography, Gender Matters*, and *Related Courses*. There is also a search form at the bottom of the page that can be set to search the entire site or discrete units of it. Looking at individual regions—for instance, Africa—there is a list of the English-speaking countries of the area (Ghana, Namibia, Nigeria, South Africa, and

Zimbabwe), a list of authors tied to those nations, and separate categories for economics, geography, history, politics, religion, and so forth that together comprise a broad contextual treatment of the region. In addition, there is a separate bibliography for the entire area.

Much of the contextual treatment is of a general nature and is culled from standard sources such as the *CIA World Factbook*, but there are also on occasion original scholarly essays. The thematic sections present an equally broad array of material. Of particular interest is the in-depth treatment of postcolonial theory, which includes separate sections for *Themes & Issues*, *Theorists*, *Terms*, *Gender Matters*, *Historical Contexts*, *Symbol & Image*, *Bibliography*, and a concluding *Overview*. Despite the breadth of the site, one item that is conspicuous in its absence is any mention of Canada and Canadian literature as fitting in the realm of postcolonialism. An excellent site for filling this lacunae is the **Canadian Literature Archive** at **http://canlit.st-john.umanitoba. ca/Canlitx/Framed_Version/CanlitF.html**.

Postmodern Theory, Culture Studies and Hypertext

http://www.marist.edu/humanities/ english/eculture.html

According to one perspective, hypertext and postmodernism are the future of English lit-erature. This engaging site maintains this futuristic outlook and is the work of Professor Tom Goldpaugh, Department of English, Marist University.

Professor Goldpaugh abjures definitions so that perhaps the best way of describing the site is to say that it serves as a kind of buffet of postmodern practice. As befits a site dedicated to hypertext there are numerous embedded links throughout, but there is also a definite structure to the site, consisting of three main divisions: *Hypertext Theory and Sites*, *Hypertext Projects and Fiction*, and *Postmodern, Cyber and Cultural Studies*. The first division explores the dimensions and implications of hypertext as a tool for writing and communication. The second division furnishes numerous examples of hypertext fiction where hypertext is self-consciously employed as means of expanding the bounds of fiction. The final category, dealing with cyber culture and postmodernism, links to sites that try to make sense and draw out the broader philosophical implications of the diffusion of electronic communications. Links within the divisions are arranged alphabetically, but what makes this site stand out is not only the care expended in the selection of links but the detailed and thoughtful annotation of each of the links. Bald titles of sites will not be found here. The most telling attribute of Professor Goldpaugh's annotations is that his enthusiasm is infectious, and it is difficult to resist visiting many of the sites he recommends.

Foreign Languages

The web has a universal presence, and although underdeveloped or Third World nations are not as well-represented as developed nations, there is virtually not a spot on the globe that is not signified on the web. As a consequence, the web is a great teaching tool for the diversity of nations and peoples.

A special beneficiary of the emergence of the web is foreign language instruc tion. If one is studying French, for instance, it is one thing to go to the library once a week and read *Le Match*, yet it is altogether a different thing to read a French newspaper like *Libération* on the web daily. Moreover, it is even a grander thing to virtually travel to foreign lands and to savor the sights and cultural landmarks of a nation. Foreign language instruction is a much more vivid and engaging enterprise owing to the web.

This chapter obviously cannot hope to cover the many languages present on the web. The focus will be on those languages, mostly Western, that are most frequently taught on campuses. The aim will be less on language instruction proper as opposed to sites that offer a broad venue to the various cultures in question.

http://www.june29.com/HLP

This massive site with over 1700 links is the creation of Tyler Chambers, Boston. He bills the site as a "comprehensive catalog of langu-age related Internet resources." It is fully searchable and is divided into a number of categories, including *Languages & Literature, Schools & Institutions, Linguistics Resources, Commercial Resources, Organizations, Latest Additions,* and *Jobs & Internships*.

The largest and most substantial category by far is the first, devoted to *Languages & Literature*. The directory of the languages listed alone runs nine pages and ranges from *Ab-*

original Languages to *Yiddish*. In between, there is a host of rare and exotic languages such as *Dalekarlian* (a Swedish derivative), *Manx* (a Gaelic/Celtic dialect), *Occitan* (an ancient in-termediary between Iberic tongues and French), and *Urdu* (an Indian language derived from Persian, Arabic, and Sanskrit). Obviously, the more widely used languages proportionally havea greater share of resources devoted to them. Almost all of the sites for each of the languages have strong audio components so that one can hear the language and practice pronunciation.

Many of the other categories are also quite extensive. The category for *Schools and Insti-tutions* offers a valuable directory of language schools and university programs. Likewise, the category *Commercial Resources* lists a broad variety of language software programs and translation services. One other item of import linked at the top of the page is the remarkable **AltaVista Translation Service** at **http:// babelfish.altavista.digital.com**. The AltaVista search engine offers computerized translations of any web site or url in English to either German, Spanish, French, Italian and Por-tuguese, or vice versa. The machine rendered translations are often crude, and are certainly inappropriate for literature, yet they are aston-ishingly quick. The machine translations also furnish a good test for polishing one's own translation skills.

A Web of On-line Grammars
http://www.facstaff.bucknell.edu/ rbeard/grammars.html

This site is not as massive as the previous one, but may be more useful for that very reason. It is the creation of Professor Robert Beard,

Director of Russian and Linguistics Programs, Bucknell University. Grammar indicates the internal structural relationships within a language and thereby stands at the forefront of language instruction and acquisition.

Professor Beard has compiled introductory grammars for approximately sixty languages. He lists them in straight alphabetical order, and obviously some are more elaborate and substantial than others. However, all the links have been carefully selected for content, and each provides at least an introduction to the language in question. Many provide much more. For instance, Professor Beard's contribution on Russian grammar is a model of both concision and high information content. In what he dubs *Preliminaries*, he introduces the Cyrillic alphabet and general spelling and pronunciation rules, and then advances to separate meaty sections devoted to *The Russian Verb*, *The Russian Noun*, *The Russian Adjective*, *The Russian Pronoun*, and the *Russian Preposition*.

Many of the individual grammars are equipped with sound, and even if there is no intention of dedicating oneself to a foreign language, it is nonetheless interesting to sample the variety. Another fine site that advocates the incorporation of the web into foreign language instruction is **Language Interactive** at **http://www.fln.vcu.edu/cgi/interact.html**.

Euroseek
http://www.euroseek.net

For better or worse, the bulk of foreign languages taught in academic departments are European or of European origin. EuroSeek is a multilingual search engine that is an ideal launching place for exploring Europe. The European continent is interpreted in a broad way here so as to embrace Central and Eastern Europe, Russia, and Turkey.

The homepage features a query form that can be limited either by region or by language. To give an idea of the flexibility of this search

tool, there are forty different language choices. The left margin of the page also offers a number of options, including Internet yellow pages and business directory, a large subject directory ranging from advertising to weather, and a massive set of news links listing over 2,800 sites in 145 countries. For instance, Austria alone boasts sixteen news sites encompassing not only Vienna but also Salzburg, Innsbruck, Graz, and so forth. This is a marvelous way to practice and enhance language skills.

The homepage also has an icon that links to the European Union. Located here is information concerning the progress of the European Union and a detailed explanation of its activities and administrative structure. There is an equal amount of economic and business information, and it is clear that strenuous efforts are being made to encourage exploration of Europe as a seat of investment and business opportunities. Too often students and citizens of the United States envisage Europe merely in cultural terms limited to literature and the arts. Although EuroSeek and the European Union contain numerous links to high culture, they also show another vital side to Europe, and that is its economic dynamism. These sites also reveal that Europeans are just as caught up as Americans with mastering and employing the web as an information resource.

HAPAX: French Resources on the Web
http://ripley.wo.sbc.edu/departmental/french/hapax

There are any number of sites devoted to France and things French, but Hapax is particularly attractive in the way it is geared to the student. This site, created by Professor Angelo Metzidakis, Department of French, Sweet Briar College, does not claim to be comprehensive but offers a broad and carefully selective overview of French society and culture. Hapax is divided into twenty-eight broad categories. Among the more interesting are those dedicated to *Art and Architecture*, *Culture*, *History*, *Language*, *Literature*, *Political Science and Economy*, *Science*, *Tourism*, and so forth. The category on language, for example, lists sixteen different links to a broad variety of language lessons and language games, ranging from the novice to the advanced user.

Outside the language sources there are hundreds of links that flesh out the image of France. Moreover, there is a great deal of invaluable information for those contemplating a visit to France or those who plan to study there. Not only can one select sites to see, but one can also draw up a detailed itinerary of how to travel to those sites, where to stay, and so forth. The links tend to be fairly evenly divided between sites of French and U.S. origin, which again underlines the point that one does not necessarily have to be a French speaker to enjoy and benefit from Hapax. More advanced students with an interest in nineteenth century French history are recommended to visit a magnificent and massive French site comparable to the Library of Congress', *American Memory Project*; the Bibliothèque Nationale's **Gallica** at **http://gallica.bnf.fr**.

German Studies Trails on the Web

http://www.uncg.edu/~lixlpurc/german.html

This fine site is maintained by Professor Andreas Lixl, Department of German, University of North Carolina at Greensboro. At the top of the page there is a wide selection of German language search engines, followed by an assortment of ten topical areas exploring German

culture and society. The categories include *Language & Civilization*, *Arts & Humanities*, *Science & Technology*, *Education & Research*, *Economics*, and so forth. The largest category, and most relevant for our purposes, is that focused on *Sprache und Landeskunde* (language and culture), which covers both high and popular culture and comprehends not only Germany but Austria, the Swiss Helvetic Confederation, and Liechtenstein. Located here is diverse information on geography, film, newspapers and magazines, politics, religion, and Germany's burgeoning Internet culture. There are also numerous lesson plans and exercises for learning German.

The remaining categories contain numerous items of interest and range over the full terrain of German studies. Of particular interest is a group of other Internet activities initiated by Professor Lixl and which he locates under the category of *German Internet Project*. "German Studies Trails on the Web" is just one aspect of this larger project, which in effect constitutes a graded or step-by-step introduction to the German language starting at the most elementary level—*KinderWeb. Links for All Ages*. For a somewhat flashier introduction to the contemporary German scene see, **The German Way**, a massive resource located at **http://www.german-way.com/german**.

Japan, My Japan! A Guide to Japan

http://lang.nagoya-u.ac.jp/%7Ematsuoka/Japan.html

Japan's economic dynamism has clearly made

it a world power, and consequently there has been a growing interest in acquiring Japanese language skills and understanding its culture and society.

This engaging site is the work of Professor Mitsuharu Matsuoka (we have included his "American Authors on the Web" in the previous chapter), Nagoya University, Japan. The site is divided into ten categories, including *WWW Servers, General Resources, Search Engines and Directories, Culture & Society, Mass Media, Travel and Sightseeing, Tokyo, Literature, Language,* and *Miscellaneous Resources.* Links are listed in simple alphabetical order under each category, and there is virtually no commentary on the individual links. In short, for selection purposes there is not much guide other than the title alone. For instance, the category under *Language* lists more than eighty links, ranging from the most basic Japanese for travelers to advanced instruction in a variety of Japanese dialects. In order to choose the most appropriate or interesting site, it is necessary to browse the entire list, and then with a bit of guesswork choose accordingly. On the other hand, for many categories, such as *Tokyo* and *Travel and Sightseeing,* the links are largely self-explanatory. All in all, Professor Matsuoka has done an admirable job of opening windows from which to view Japan. For those more interested exclusively in Japanese language instruction see the elaborate multimedia site **The Japanese Tutor** at **http://web.missouri.edu/c563382**.

---

http://solar.rtd.utk.edu/friends/home.html

This pioneering work is jointly maintained by Greg Cole, Director of the Center for International Networking Initiative, University of Tennessee, and Natasha Bulashova, Office of Grants and Special Information in the Institute of Biochemistry and Physiology of Microor-

ganisms in the Russian Academy of Science, Pushchino, Moscow region. They feel the Internet is an ideal means of fostering friendship and better relations between the United State and the states of the former Soviet Union.

The site contains a huge number of links, but it is well-organized and relatively easy to navigate. The homepage lists the site's main sections as *Culture, Commerce/Business, Education/Science, Funding/Exchange, Language//Cyrillic, Life/Family, News/History, Telecommunications,* and *Tourism/Travel.* Each of these sections in turn is divided into a number of topical categories. In addition, there are other sections devoted to a chatline and listserv, outreach projects initiated by "Friends and Partners," and there is also a handy keyword search form at the bottom of the page.

Of particular interest is the section on language, which has separate entries for *Dictionaries, Study Programs, Tutorials,* and *Cyrillic Text.* With regard to the latter entry one of the obvious problems involved in the translation between English and Russian is that they have their own alphabets. There are, however, numerous guidelines and software packages presented here detailing how to Russify text and vice versa. I was particularly impressed with the section on *Life/Family,* which deals with day-to-day experience such as hobbies, cookery, women's issues and the like. Not to be missed is the expansive subsection *Communities in Russia,* which furnishes a massive set of links (the index alone runs twenty-eight pages) to cities, towns, and regions throughout Russia and the Newly Independent States. This section offers a marvelous entry to the diversity of the former Soviet republics.

Sí, Spain
http://www.SiSpain.org/

The idea for this site originated with Dr. José Luis Pardos, Spanish Ambassador to Canada, and is currently maintained under the auspices of the Directorate General of Cultural Affairs of the Spanish Foreign Ministry. The site is divided into sixteen separate categories, including *Geography, Population and Society, History, Language and Culture, Politics and Public Administration, Economy and Trade, Education, Science and Technology, The Media, Traveling to Spain, Spanish Courses on the Internet, Other Web Sites in or about Spain,* and so forth. Most of the divisions boast origianl material, such as the history category which features a descriptive timetable of Spain's past.

There are all kinds of interesting nuggets spread throughout the site. For instance, the section on traveling points out that, "Spaniards tend to get up later in the morning and stay out later at night than the rest of European neighbors" and that "tipping is a great tradition in Spain." These are good things to know. The section on Internet-accessible language instruction is a bit weak. However, the category devoted to other Spanish web sites is thorough and extensive. In addition to listing numerous sites offering language instruction, there are also expansive links to tourism and the regional states of Spain, culinary specialties, bull fighting, and a huge index to Spanish fiestas. This handsome site encourages browsing, and well conveys the spirit and flavor of Spain. For those more purely interested in Spanish language instruction there is a marvelous magazine out of Birkbeck College, London, **Tecla: Texts for Learners and Teachers of Spanish at http://www.bbk.ac.uk/Departments/Spanish/TeclaHome.html**. It also must be kept in mind that Latin America is by far the most populous Spanish-speaking region. A marvelous site for the area is **LANIC: Latin America Information Network at http://www.lanic.utexas.edu**.

Less Commonly Taught Languages Project

http://carla.acad.umn.edu/lctl/lctl.html

This ingenious site is the creation of the Center for Advanced Research on Language Acquisition, University of Minnesota. It is, in effect, a clearinghouse for language instruction, excepting English, French, German, and Spanish.

Although the site is divided into a number of different categories, there are two that I feel yield the most useful information. The category *Course Offerings for Less Commonly Taught Languages* is a database that lists 292 separate languages, indicating where they are taught in the United States and Canada. More than 2000 institutions are represented. For instance, selecting the Amharic language reveals that there are only five institutions in the U.S. that offer courses (Foreign Service Institute, Harvard, Howard, Chicago, and University of California, San Diego).

The second category, dubbed *Ask the Experts*, lists native speakers and others proficient in less commonly taught languages who have volunteered to field questions on their particular language via e-mail. For most languages there are a choice of experts from whom to choose. This is an ideal site for those considering taking up a less commonly taught language or simply interested in exploring the numerous opportunities for those with special language skills.

Music and Dance

In the simplest sense, music can be defined as the art of organizing sounds. Music so defined is evident in all societies and all levels of culture. On a similar plane, dance can be defined as the art of patterned movement with the movement usually determined by musical accompaniment. Although music and dance are rooted in folk culture, the emphasis in this chapter will not be on popular variants but rather on those primarily Western forms (usually taught in institutions of higher education) that have achieved the level of high art. In short, we are speaking of the classical musical heritage, opera, ballet, and jazz.

Music, in particular, has benefited from the multimedia capacities of the web. One not only reads about music and musicians, but one can often hear them also. As a consequence, there has been an explosive growth in the number of web sites devoted to music. Owing to the richness of the material the aim here will be to sketch only the broad outlines of the field.

Worldwide Internet Music Resources

http://www.music.indiana.edu/music_resources/

This massive and comprehensive site arrives courtesy of the William and Gayle Cook Music Library, Indiana University. The thousands of links are heavily weighted toward Western classical music, but at the same time other cultures and traditions, including popular music, are well represented.

The site is divided into nine broad categories, consisting of *Individual Musicians (All Genres) and Popular Groups, Groups and Ensembles (Except Popular), Other Sites Related to Performance, Composers and Composition, Genres and Types of Music, Research and Study, The Commercial World of Music, Journals and Magazines,* and *General and Miscellaneous*. Each of the categories in turn is subdivided into a number of topical areas. For instance, *Genres and Types of Music* is divided into more than thirty areas, ranging from *Ambient/Digital Music* to *Women Composers and Women's Music*. The section devoted to composition links to over 120 composers, and the *Research and Study* area accesses not only schools and departments of music but also online databases, instrument collections, professional societies and other scholarly resources. The subsection on *Musicology and Music History* alone lists forty-one sites. In addition, there is a good deal of practical advice under the category of *The Commercial World of Music*, offering information concerning agents, music publishers, copyright, and other essential services. In sum, the site covers a lot of terrain, but its effective organization makes it a managable and rewarding venture.

Early Music FAQ

http://www.medieval.org/emfaq

This engaging site is maintained by Todd Michel McComb, an independent scholar, San Francisco. McComb defines Early Music easily enough as "Western music of the Medieval, Renaissance, and Baroque eras." Much of the site is devoted to reviews and recommendations of various recordings so as to orient the reader (and potential listener) to the broad outlines of early music.

Early music is divided into four separate eras: *Plainchant* (most commonly thought of as Gregorian Chants); *Medieval*; *Renaissance*; and *Baroque*. Despite the focus on individual recordings, the distinctiveness and innovations of each era are well developed. Throughout, there is a solid descriptive narrative and a clear indication of the historical progression of music for each period. For instance, McComb's treatment of the Renaissance begins with the French composers Gilles Binchois (c. 1400-1460) and Guillaume Dufay (1397-1474) and concludes with the Italian Carlo Gesualdo (c. 1561-1613). In between these landmarks is an extensive tour of European composition and musicianship comprehending not only France and Italy but also Spain, England, Belgium and Germany.

In addition to the historical overview, McComb furnishes information on performers and orchestras specializing in Early Music and also provides numerous links to sites that deal in some way with Early Music. The virtue of this site is that a high percentage of the material is original and although it is presented in a highly scholarly manner, no assumptions are made that the audience has any previous knowledge of Early Music.

http://www.jsbach.org

There are far too many composers and musicians on the web to be able to focus on individuals. However, an exception is made for Bach not only because of his towering achievements, but also because this is a model web site. It was created by Jan Hanford, musician and webmaster, Oakland, California, and Professor Jan Koster, Department of Linguistics, University of Groningen, Groningen, the Netherlands.

The site is extensive and boasts a high percentage of original material, yet owing to its superior organization it is easy to navigate. The homepage presents a number of different options the first of which is entitled *His Life*, and is subdivided into sections devoted to *Biography*, *Bibliography*, *Tourist Guide*, *Portraits*, and *Timeline*. Each section gives evidence of careful research, and the bibliography is particularly impressive.

The heart of the site, however, consists of two closely related sections dubbed *Complete Works* and *Recommended (or Not) Recordings*. These sections in effect function as a database of Bach's prodigious output. Individual pieces are searchable either through title, keyword, instrument, category (Church Cantatas, Concertos, and Orchestral Suites, Instrumental and Chamber Works, etc.), or BWV number (Bach Werke-Verzeichnis, the cataloging convention

for ordering Bach's works). The depth of the index is truly stunning, and clicking on an individual piece retrieves numerous recordings with full data on the recordings and evaluation of quality. Toward the bottom of the page there is a comprehensive list of additional Bach sites and a catalog of Bach's music available over the web in digitized form. This site is not to be missed by anyone who has an interest in Bach or simply takes pleasure in exploring meticulously well-crafted web productions.

http://www.classical.net

Classical music has a somewhat ambiguous definition. On the one hand, it can be taken for the whole sweep of the high-culture Western musical heritage. On the other hand, it refers to the more narrowly circumscribed period of classical composition proper, which flourished from approximately 1750-1820. This huge site encompasses the entire sweep, but its inclusion here is owing to its particular strength on post-Baroque music.

The site is maintained by the tireless L. D. Lampson, and the principal audience he seeks is the student or listener who is new to classical music. However, even seasoned connoisseurs will find much of interest here. The site is divided into six primary categories: *Basic Repertoire List*; *Classical CD Buying Guide*; *Composer's Works & Data*; *Reviews & Articles*; and *Classical Music Links*. Lampson's idea of basic repertoire is rather expansive. The list is divided into periods—*Medieval, Renaissance, Baroque, Classicism, Romanticism, 20th Century, Modern*—and each period is aligned with composers characteristic of the era. The romantic period, for example, comprehends eighty composers, starting with Adam and ending with Wolf. Each individual composer is then linked not only to sites furnishing additional information but also to an overview of recommended recordings. In short, the basic repertoire is both dense and expansive. With the exception of the reviews (which feature those other than Lampson's) and the external links section, the remainder of the site refers back to basic repertoire category. The section on external links is a marvel in itself and contains numerous subdivisions charting the world of classical music. Another worthwhile site dedicated to the classical music heritage, yet which is pitched at a more elementary level, is **The World Wide Web Virtual Library: Classical Music** at **http://www.gprep.pvt.k12. md.us/classical**.

Kalvos and Damian's Music Bazaar—New Music Composers from Around the World

http://www.maltedmedia.com/kalvos/

Contemporary or new music draws heavily from the Western classical heritage but is certainly not strictly limited to it. The best that can be said is that it is an amalgam of music traditions, and that most often has strong avant-garde leanings. It can also be added that the audience for this music is comparatively small bu intensely devoted.

This site is a good illustration of the latter. The site is the creation of the composers Dennis Báthory-Kitsz and David Gunn (a.k.a Kalvos and Damian), and it is an extension of their radio program broadcast by WGDR FM 91.1, Goddard College, Plainfield, Vermont. The site is divided into numerous sections,

including *Guest Composer Index, Worldwide Composer Resources, The Graffiti Page* (a mix of multimedia sounds and images), *Top 100 Favorites, Essays by Composers, Worldwide Composer Pages, Recording Label Index*, and so forth. Each of the sections shows a somewhat different dimension of the new music movement. As one might imagine, much of the music is experimental in nature and not readily available. It is a good thing that Báthory-Kitsz and Gunn list a number of small labels that market new music. However, even better is that they make available hundreds of sound files to sample the music.

The music itself offers an astonishing range of sounds and styles. One frequent characteristic, perhaps owing to the music's obscurity, is that the titles of works and the works themselves are often humorous or, at least, sardonic. For instance, there are a number of featured essays by David Gunn with titles such as *Suffix Perturbation, Day of Atonalment, The Drool Chute*, and many others in a similar vein. Another aspect of the new music is its close alliance with other avant-garde art forms such as dance, performance art, and experimental literature. In this regard, it is entirely appropriate that Báthory-Kitsz and Gunn would characterize their site as a "bazaar." Even if one is not inclined toward new music this site is a worthwhile stop and is a fine example of the kind of platform the web offers for experimental and avant-garde works.

Operabase

http://www.operabase.com

This fine site is the creation of Mike Gibb, a software engineer working in London, England. As one might imagine, the site is devoted to classical opera. The layout is elaborate but easy to follow, and includes a number of interesting features.

The site is divided into two main sections: *Composers and Their Operas*; and *Opera Houses and Festivals*. The first category offers an alphabetical list of 130 composers, and a separate list of 278 operas. There is also a combined chronological timeline of composers and works. Gibb's industry and ingenuity are most evident in the way in which he has annotated individual entries. For instance, clicking on "M" under composers retrieves a list of fourteen, ranging from Maillart to Musorgsky. Moreover, he has constructed a detailed legend indicating what kind of materials are available for each entry. The legend reads: *bio* (biography); *works* (list of works); *pic* (picture); *syn* (synopsis); *lib* (libretto); *disc* (discography); *back* (background); and *perf* (performance history.) In addition, there is a separate icon for attached sound files. Many composers will draw from only a few of the material types, but major operatic composers, such as Mozart, Rossini, or Verdi are well-represented by each type. All tolled, there is a tremendous variety and depth of information. Gibb's schema of opera houses and festivals, which includes more than 400 individual sites, is equally ingenious in that it consists of an elaborate series of clickable maps that allows one to progressively focus on a specific region or area. Finally, Gibbs is very gracious in acknowledging the various links and sources which comprise the database. Another excellent source focused on the current opera scene is **Operanet** at http://www.culturekiosque.com/opera/.

http://www.novia.net/~jlw/

This beautifully illustrated site is the creation of Jim Williams, a professional ballet photographer. Music obviously always accompanies ballet, but the emphasis here is on dance.

Through a series of photographic essays Williams stresses the rigorous training and mechanics of dance. One of the essays also features a portfolio of shots of a contemporary performance of Mikhail Fokine's epochal ballet *Les Sylphides*. Williams dedication to dance is evident not only in the artistry of his photographs but also in the accompanying narrative.

Of particular interest to the ballet novice is an exhibit dubbed *The Electric Ballerina*. The exhibit consists of a series of QuickTime videos illustrating fundamental ballet steps and movements such as the *fouétte* (leg-swinging spin), *saut de chat* (leap), *jeté en tournant* (leaping half-turn in midair), *pas de deux* (steps for two), and *arabesques* (graceful, classical poses.) In addition, there are separate sections devoted to *Dance Quotations*, *Dance Humor*, and a highly sophisticated *Dance Photography Notebook*. At the tail-end of the page there is also a very limited, but carefully selected list of links to other ballet sites.

Williams has done a marvelous job of melding the traditional craftsmanship of ballet to the most recent multimedia techniques and platforms, yet one eccentric aspect of the site is that male dancers are virtually absent. For a much broader set of dance links, not limited exclusively to ballet see **Dance Links** at **http://www.dancer.com/dance.links**. Although the above site is strong on modern/contemporary dance, there is not a single site that attempts to cover this art in a comprehensive manner. However, a site of particular interest devoted to one of the giants of modern dance is the homepage for **Merce Cunningham** at **http://www.merce.org/**.

Theatricopia

An abundance of links and more for Musical Theatre fans

http://www.saintmarys.edu/~jhobgood/Jill/theatre.html

Musical theater is obviously a hybrid that combines drama and music, and often dance as well. This clever site well captures the multiform nature of the medium, and is the creation of Jill Hobgood, Lecturer and Librarian, Saint Mary's College, Notre Dame, Indiana.

At the top of the page the category *Shows* lists alphabetically almost 200 musical theater productions with a web presence. The shows range from the intriguingly titled *Butt Pirates of the Caribbean* to *Miss Saigon* to *West Side Story*. Other categories that follow, include *Performers, Composers and Lyricists, Other Musical Theatre Professionals* (producers, choreographers, designers), *Magazines, Newsletters and Reviews, Recordings and Stores, Multimedia and Discographies, Lyrics and Libretti, Awards* (Tony, Playbill, Critics' Circle Awards, etc.)*General Theatre Links and More*, and several others. Most of the categories have a number of topical subdivisions followed by an alphabetical register of sites. The amount of commentary from one link to another or even different categories varies a great deal. It is evident from the commentary that Ms. Hobgood is particularly keen on reviews and recordings, and accordingly lavishes a great deal of attention on these topics. It is equally evident that her enthusiasm is matched by her knowledge and comprehensive grasp of the world of musical theater. Other excellent sites for musical theater are **Virtual Bro adway** at **http://www.geocities.com/~trenews/vbintro.htm** and **Better Living Through ShowTunes** at **http://www.bettershowtunes.com**.

WNUR-FM JazzWeb

http://www.acns.nwu.edu/jazz

Jazz is oft referred to as America's classical music, and this marvelous site comes courtesy of Joe Germuska and Northwestern University's innovative and eclectic WNUR radio station.

The site is divided into a number of categories including *Styles of Jazz* (hypermap and essays), *Artists* (bios, discographies, reviews), *Performance* (festivals, venues, reviews, regional jazz info), *Jazz Instruments, Media* (radio, television, press), *Jazz Art* (jazz inspired literature, painting, photography), *Jazz Education and Musicianship, Jazz Retailers on the Net, Jazz Labels on the Net*, and *Other Jazz Resources on the Internet*. Interspersed throughout the various categories are numerous essays and audio files. Particularly impressive is the first category dubbed *Styles*, which, in effect, offers a hypertext timeline and history of the evolution of jazz. The hypermap is laid out like a flowchart and opens with ragtime and advances to New Orleans, Kansas City, Swing, Bebop, and all the way to the present. Although the narrative for each division and era is yet to be filled, the chart presents a striking image of the sweep and development of jazz. The chart is complemented by the *Performance* category, which has hundreds of links to jazz artists and legends ranging from Louis Armstrong to Billie Holliday to contemporary performers like Wynton Marsalis.

Jazz recordings are infrequently big sellers and consequently are often difficult to locate. However, the advent of the Internet has made the situation much easier, and Germuska furnishes a good list of Internet accessible retailers and record labels. In addition, there is a carefully selected set of links featuring jazz. Of particular note is the remarkable series of lectures delivered at the Kennedy Center by the renowned pianist, Dr. Billy Taylor, grouped under the title **What Is Jazz?** at **http://town.hall.org/Archives/radio/KennedyTaylor/**.

Ethnomusicology, Folk Music, and World Music

http://www.lib.washington.edu/music/world.html

Ethnomusicology, or literally the study of music from different cultures, is a rapidly growing field. Not long ago ethnomusicology was generally referred to as exotic music, but with growing acceptance it has lost that tag. Today ethnic music or world music inhabits that huge realm that comprehends all forms of music outside that of Western European high culture.

This particular site comes courtesy of the University of Washington's Music Library and is maintained by John Gibbs. The site has a simple and straightforward design and is divided into four main sections: *Organizations, Institutions, Archives; Bibliography, Periodicals & Online Publications; Recordings: Labels and Distributors*; and *Sites by Geographical Region*. Each of the divisions contains items of interest, but the vast bulk of the resources and links are located in the latter geographic category. Its subdivisions include *British/Irish/American Folk Music, Native American, Asia,*

Middle East and North Africa, Eastern Europe and Russia, Europe, Africa, Latin America, the Caribbean, South America, and *Oceania*. Each of these geographic headings lists a number of links that range from sound files to performers to bibliographies and databases. Virtually every corner of the globe is represented, and it is fascinating to browse and listen to the myriad varieties of music and instrumentation. For a more purely scholarly approach to ethnomusicology see **The Society for Ethnomusicology** at **http://www.indiana.edu/~ethmusic/**.

Philosophy and Religion

Philosophy and religion represent two different ways of knowing, and in certain guises it is difficult to separate the two. At the highest realms both are concerned with the acquisition of knowledge and wisdom. A large portion of each field is also devoted to defining morality. On the other hand, the day-to-day practice and observance of religion is generally unsystematic, whereas contemporary philosophy is almost wholly confined to the academy and often employs a highly technical language and forms of argumentation in addressing questions. Indeed, philosophy today is fragmented into a number of competing schools and branches such as ethics, symbolic logic, epistemology, and so forth.

Emphasis here will be on highlighting some of the major philosophical camps. On the religious side there are far too many denominations and creeds to offer adequate coverage. Stress will therefore be placed on sites that treat religion in a comparative manner.

Guide to Philosophy on the Internet

http://www.earlham.edu/~peters/philinks.htm

This vast and impressive site is the work of Professor Peter Suber, Philosophy Department, Earlham College.

At the top of the page is a search engine dubbed *Hippias*, which not only searches all the links within Suber's guide but also searches a number of other prominent Internet guides and links to philosophy. In short, it surveys thousands of links and for this reason should be used with some caution. For instance, typing in "heidegger" retrieves almost 250 hits. Not only is this number a bit overwhelming, but it is also often difficult to see the relevance of the retrieved items to the search term. Despite the drawbacks, *Hippias* is a powerful search tool for canvassing the Internet. Other substantial and important categories include *Guides, Philosophers, Topics, Etexts, Bibliographies, Dictionaries, Quotations, Teaching/Learning,*

and numerous others. Specially recommended sites are designated with a red star, and many of the links are furnished with a brief explanatory note. The *Guides* section features general links to philosophy, and is broken down into separate languages. There are more than sixty general guides listed in English, and eleven of those are awarded special honors.

The largest section is devoted to web sites for specific philosophers. Individuals are listed alphabetically and range from Abelard to Wittgenstein. The topics section focuses on different schools of thought (deconstruction, critical theory, actualism, etc.) and various branches of philosophical enquiry (ethics, logic, epistemology, etc.). In addition, there is a rich mine of both historical and contemporary electronic texts and a number of distinguished online bibliographies and databases. Another very fine Australian site with a superior topical organization is **Philosophy in Cyberspace** at **http://www-personal.monash.edu.au/~dey/phil.**

http://www.utm.edu/research/iep

As the title implies this is a reference work. It is maintained by Professor James Fieser, Department of Philosophy, University of Tennessee at Martin.

The site is divided into three sections: *Timeline; Philosophy Text Collection;* and *Key Words.* The collection of online texts is not impressive, but it is more than compensated by the timeline and keyword indexes. The former features a chronological list of major philosophers and schools of philosophy in the West with links back to the encyclopedia. The timeline is divvied up into broad periods (*Ancient, Medieval, Renaissance, Modern,* etc.) and then broken down into topical categories characteristic of the period under review. In short, the chart offers a convenient overview of the sweep of Western philosophy. The keyword index offers a alphabetical list of significant philosophers and philosophical terms, ranging from *a priori* to *Xenophon*. Many of the more pivotal terms are marked by multiple entries. For instance, there are over twenty-five terms grouped under the concept of *ethics*. Individual entries are often quite substantial and in effect are mini-essays that offer a concise review and guide to further reading. However, like any undertaking of this sort there are bound to be holes and occasional oddities. There is little here on contemporary Continental philosophy, which no doubt reflects Professor Fieser and his colleagues areas of expertise. Nonetheless, there is an impressive amount of information available through the encyclopedia. Over time no doubt its content will be fleshed out. An interesting comparable web site worth a visit is the **Stanford Encyclopedia of Philosophy** at **http://plato.stanford.edu**.

http://209.63.222.24:80/dstorm/plato

This beautiful site is the work of D. Anthony Storm, a professional web designer with a keen interest in philosophy. Plato was arguably the greatest of the Greek philosophers: student and mouthpiece for Socrates and teacher of Aristotle.

The site is divided into a number of categories, including *Commentary, Introduction, Methodology, Bibliography, Links*, and *Gallery*. There is considerable original narrative throughout starting with the *Introduction,* which surveys a number of Plato's and Socrates' most distinctive ideas. However, the heart of the site is located under the rubric, *Commentary*. Here Storm groups Plato's works into three periods—early, middle, and late. Each of the periods has its own distinctive traits, and

Storm includes all of Plato's works, even a few where the authorship is questionable. Not only is a concise commentary attached to each of the writings, but also the full texts are available in both Greek and English translation.

All tolled, there are thirty separate works represented, ranging from the early Socratic dialogs such as the *Apology* to the later works such as the *Laws*. The lengthiest original contribution by far is located under the category of *Methodology*. The essay offers an intricate account of Plato's practice of writing and composition. On the other hand, the *Bibliography* and *Links* sections are very selective, and focus only on the highlights. Finally, the *Gallery* features sculpted images of Plato and Socrates. There are a number of other fine sites devoted to Greek and ancient philosophy. Prior to Plato, there were a number of contending schools of philosophy. An fine site dedicated to the **Presocratic Philosophers** is at **http://www.forthnet.gr/presocratics/indeng. htm**. There is also an excellent page for **Aristotle** at **http://www.baylor.edu/~Scott_ Moore/aristotle.html**.

St. Thomas Aquinas

http://www.niagara.edu/~loughlin/ index.html

It is a great leap in time from the ancients to the high Middle Ages, yet at least in the realm of philosophy there is a strong commonality. After all, Aquinas and Thomistic philosophy are grounded on a synthesis of Aristotelian and Christian thought.

This site is the work of Stephen Loughlin, a recently minted Philosophy Ph.D. from the University of Toronto. The arrangement of the site is different from many others, in that it is not broken up into topical categories but is rather presented in the way of a running narrative. At the top of the page there is chronology of Aquinas' life. The two traits that stand out are his devotion to the Dominican order, against determined parental opposition, and his enormous capacity for work and scholarship.

The remainder of the site offers a combination of translations of St. Thomas' works and contemporary commentary and discussion of those works. It is perfectly fitting that the mix of sites is both philosophical and religious, more properly Catholic. There are links to a complete online version of the monumental *Summa Theologiae,* as well as the remarkable commentary of Father Walter Farrell, *A Companion to the Summa,* that weighs in at a hefty 1,836 pages. In between, there are many other concise and informative items about Aquinas' thought and influence, which continues to this day. For those interested in earlier thought of the late antique and medieval periods, see the **James J. O'Donnell Home Page** at **http://ccat.ssas.upenn.edu/jod/**, or the rich collection of texts at **The Internet Medieval Sourcebook** at **http://www.fordham.edu/halsall/sbook.html**.

http://www.orst.edu/~uzgalisw/302

Professor William Uzgalis, Department of Philosophy, Oregon State University, created this site for a survey he teaches of philosophy between the sixteenth and eighteenth centuries.

The site is divided into two sections, the *Era* and the *Course,* of which the latter is not really relevant to the outsider. However, the former is divided into a number of sections of general interest. The first significant section is entitled *Stories and Themes,* which offers an original and succinct overview of the evolution of ideas over the period. For instance, Uzgalis discusses the turn away from the Renaissance veneration of the classics and the discovery of new sources of philosophical inspiration, such as the growth of science and mathematics and the discovery of the New World. Other major themes include the Reformation and the rise of empiricism and skepticism.

The second outstanding section is entitled *The Philosophers* and features a selection of the most noted philosophers of the period. The individual philosophers are grouped by country, and then listed chronologically. For instance, the eleven philosophers selected for France, range from *Michel de Montaigne* to *Jean Jacques Rousseau.* Each philosopher is furnished with a brief original essay summarizing their thought and contribution to philosophy. There are also generally links to other pages devoted to that particular philosopher and additional links to online texts. Unquestionably, Uzgalis has placed a great deal of energy into developing this project and the site well conveys the philosophical originality and richness of the period. However, the site also needs a serious updating, especially with regard to expanding the links to individual philosophers and texts. A good index with links for individual philosophers of the period is available at the previously cited general site "Guide to Philosophy on the Internet."

http://www.augustana.ab.ca/~janzb/continental.htm

This broad-ranging site picks up from post-Enlightenment Europe to the present. It is the creation of Professor Bruce Janz, Department of Philosophy and Interdisciplinary Studies, Augustana University College, Camrose, Alberta.

At the top of the page there is a list of comprehensive sites tagged *General Purpose Continental Philosophy Pages*. This is followed by a very useful topical arrangement, *Areas of Continental Philosophy*, that introduces a wide array of links to divergent schools, including *Critical Theory, Deconstruction, Existentialism, German Idealism, Marxism, Phenomenology, Post-Colonialism, Post-Modernism,*and so forth.

Succeeding the topical list, there is a shift in focus to individual philosophers under the categorie, *People, 19th Century & Earlier*, and *People, 20th Century*. The former ranges from Wilhelm Dilthey to Max Stirner, and the list has a heavily German flavor with particularly strong entries for Hegel, Kant, and Nietzsche. The latter category is much more extensive and ranges from Theodor Adorno to Ludwig Wittgenstein. Fortunately, Janz takes a broad view of philosophy and includes a host of figures not immediately identified with philosophy, such as Roland Barthes (literary critticism), Noam Chomsky (linguistics), Helene Cixous (feminist theory), Jacques Lacan (psychoanalysis), and many others. The end result emphasizes the catholic and interdisciplinary character of contemporary philosophical enquiry. Another fine site covering similar ground is Professor Scott Moore's **The Notebook for Contemporary Continental Philosophy** at **http://www.baylor.edu/~Scott_Moore/Continental.html**.

Contemporary American Philosophy

http://www.baylor.edu/~Scott_Moore/American.html

This site is an adjunct to the aforementioned "Notebook for Contemporary Continental Philosophy," and again is the creation of Professor Scott Moore, Department of Philosophy, Baylor University.

There are distinctive traits to American philosophy, particularly the genesis and evolution of Pragmatism. However, Moore does not limit the scope of the page to any one school and rather presents a selective list of prominent contemporary philosophers. The list includes links to pages and individual essays on *John Dewey, Jean Bethke Elshtain, Mary Ann Glendon, William James, Alasdair MacIntyre, Martha Nussbaum, Charles Sanders Peirce, Richard Rorty, Charles Taylor*, and *Cornel West*.

This is certainly a distinguished company of philosophers, but conspicuous by its absence is the lack of reference to the analytic school, which is also one of the mainstays of American philosophy. Unfortunately, there is not yet a site that treats the analytic school as a group. However, there is a distinguished periodical that treats all aspects of the analytic school, **The Electronic Journal of Analytic Philosophy** at **http:/www.phil.indiana.edu./ejap**. For the earlier Transcendental school of American philosophy, see the pages for **Ralph Waldo Emerson** and **Henry David Thoreau** at **http:// http://www.geocities.com/Athens/7687**.

Ethics Updates

http://ethics.acusd.edu/index.html

Ethics, or enquiry into the nature of morality, is one of the principal branches of philosophy, and, as this superb site makes clear, there are a host of divergent ethical perspectives and arguments.

Professor Lawrence Hinman, Department. of Philosophy, University of San Diego, maintains the site and has contributed a great deal of his own material drawn from textbooks he has authored. At the top of the page, there is a search form for browsing the entire site. Following below, the site is divided into two major categories: *Ethical Theory* and *Applied Ethics*. The former leads off with a very fine *Introduction to Moral Theory*, and there are also independent sections on *Religion and Ethics, Kant and Deontology, Aristotle and Virtue Ethics, Ethical Relativism, Ethical Egoism, Rights Theories, Gender and Moral Theory, Meta-Ethical Concerns, Utilitarianism, Contemporary Anti-Theory*, and *Race, Ethnicity, and Moral Theory*. Each of the sections stands as an independent essay and includes not only Hinman's overview and extensive bibliographic commentary but also links to articles, papers, lectures, and relevant sites. Hinman also appends a set of discussion questions at the end of each section.

The latter section devoted to applied ethics, includes sections on *Abortion, Reproductive Technologies and Bioethics, Euthanasia, Punishment and the Death Penalty, Race and Ethnicity, Gender and Sexism, Sexual Orientation, Poverty and Welfare, World Hunger, Animal Rights,* and *Environmental Ethics.* The format is somewhat different here, in that many of the links and material on display are not purely philosophical. For instance, the hot button issue of abortion presents primary evidence, such as court cases and legislation along with the views of various contending groups (e.g., NOW vs. the Catholic church) and also popular treatments of the debate. Only at the bottom of the page do the philosophers weigh in with their own arguments. Hinman's coverage of applied ethics is consistently challenging and stimulating, which applies as well to the remainder of this exemplary site.

LogicAL

Logic, Philosophy, and Artificial Life Resources

http://uu-gna.mit.edu:8001/~napoli/ LAMBDA/logical.html

Logic is another of the principal branches of philosophy. Although the practice of traditional logic as established by the ancients is still very much alive, this site attests to the many new avenues opened up to logical enquiry with the advent of the computer.

The site is maintained by S. Kritikos, who is affiliated with the electronic-based Globe-wide Network Academy. The site is divided into numerous categories, the most significant of which for the beginner is *Logic through History.* Here one finds a succinct chronolog-

ical overview of the major figures in logic, ranging from Aristotle to the computer pioneers Alan Turing and John Von Neumann. The remainder of the site is devoted to recent research in logic and its applications and includes the categories *Logic and Philosophy, Logic and Mathematics, Logic and Computation, Complexity and Information, Automata and Systems, Fuzzy Logic,* and *Artificial Intelligence and Robotics.*

In addition, there are numerous links to relevant software, companies, professional associations and the like. It is clear that Kritikos favors the more scientific and computer science orientation of research in logic, which certainly dominates the contemporary scene. However, a more traditional view of logic as reasoned argument can be accessed at Professor Garth Kemmerling's page devoted to **Logic** at **http:// people.delphicom/gkemerling/lg.fallacy/fall. htm.**

Virtual Religion Index

http://religion.rutgers.edu/links/ vrindex.html

This enormous and comprehensive site is maintained by Professor Mahlon H. Smith, Religion Department, Rutgers University.

The site is divided into eighteen geographic and topical categories that are arranged in simple alphabetical order. Examples of geo graphic categories, include *American Religions, Ancient Near Eastern Studies, East Asian Studies,* and *Greco-Roman Studies.* Topical categories include *Anthropology & Sociology of Religion, Buddhist Tradition, Christian Tradition, Comparative Religion, Ethics & Moral Values, Hindu Tradition, Islam, Philosophy & Theology,* and *Psychology of Religion.* Each of the categories in turn is divided into a number of subsections. For instance, under *Islam* there are independent sections dedicated to *General Resources, Muhammad—the Prophet, The Quran (Koran), Hadith (Oral Tradition), Shariah (Law), Shi'a, Sufis,* and *Modern Movements.* Each section possesses a number carefully selected links almost all of which contain helpful and informative annotations. Moreover, each section is treated in comparable depth so that the site boasts literally hundreds of links. The combination of outstanding organization and encyclopedic scope make this a superior site. For a more purely philosophical bent on religion, see the previously mentioned Scott Moore's **Philosophy of Religion** at **http://www.baylor.edu/~Scott_Moore/Phi_Rel_info.html**. Another appealing resource is a full-text online edition of Dr. Andrew Wilson's massive and impeccable **World Scripture: A Comparative Anthology of Sacred Texts** at **http://www.unification.net/ws**.

About the Author

Jim Millhorn (B.A., history, Knox College; M.A., modern French history, University of Oklahoma; A.B.D., modern French history, University of Iowa; M.A., library science, University of Iowa) is an assistant professor and head of Acquisitions, Northern Illinois University Libraries. He was formerly reference librarian, Minot State University and social sciences librarian, Northern Illinois University. Mr. Millhorn has explored the World Wide Web since its inception and has taught numerous workshops and instructional sessions focused on Web applications to the classroom. He maintains a lively interest in the digitization of library and research material and its impact on instruction and scholarly discourse. In addition to his library duties, Mr. Millhorn remains active in the field of modern French history and has published a number of articles.